Get Unstuck

Get Unstuck

Live With Ease

I believe in you!

Blessings,

Judy Winkler

Judy Winkler

Get Unstuck
Live With Ease

Copyright @ 2010

Get Unstuck Live With Ease may be purchased or ordered through booksellers, Amazon.com, or Sacred Life Publishers at www.SacredLife.com.
ISBN: 978-0-9728592-2-6
ISBN: 0-9728592-2-5
Library of Congress Control Number: 2010924806

Cover Design by: Miko Radcliffe at www.drawingacrowd.net

Sacred Life Publishers™
www.SacredLife.com
Printed in the United States of America

DEDICATION

This book is dedicated to my children,
Patricia, Amanda and David.
You live your lives in service and in love.
Your well-lived lives are my legacy.

To all who have ever felt stuck,
and want to live with ease!

ACKNOWLEDGMENTS

A special thanks to those who encouraged and inspired me:

To Sharon Lund, who embraced this book and held my hand through the publishing process; to Dottie Bork, who lovingly edited every word and appreciated what she read; to Geri Kowahl, who shrank my mountains into mole hills, to Patricia Young who removed the remaining mole hills with ease; to Joy Lawrence, Mark Stern, Martha Scott, Jacquie Waleski, Irene Tsatsui, Tonya Gustafson, Margrit Jolly, Helga Frietag, Dottie Bork, Patricia Pastrana, Elizabeth Ornelas and Charlie Van Valkenburgh, whose friendship, love, and laughter make my world a sweet, vibrant place.

To Dr. Kathy Hearn and Rev. Blair Tabor whose inspirational messages filled me and motivated me to live a richer, more joyful life.

To Carol Angell, and T.J. Barnes who were my safety nets when I fell, Ann-Kevin Mawn, who inspired me to stay on my spiritual path; to Miss McMillan, a teacher, who saw a swan within an ugly duckling; and to every spiritual student who has allowed me to be part of your life, and every client I have coached – thank you for that privilege.

CONTENT

Introduction xiii

Abundance 1

Acceptance 3

Accidents 5

Addiction / Alcoholism 7

Adjustment 9

Age 11

Agreement 13

Anger / Antagonism 15

Answers 17

Anxiety 19

Balance 21

Beauty 23

Being Me 25

Blame 27

Burdens / Stress 29

Business 31

Cheerfulness 33

Children 35

Claiming My Place 39

Confidence 41

Confusion 43

Courage 45

Criticism 47

Death 49

Debt 51

Depression 53

Economic Security 55

Employment 57

Enlightenment 59

Enthusiasm 61

Envy 63

Expectation 65

Eyes 67

Faith 69

Family 71

Fatigue 73

Forgiving 77

Freedom 79

Friends 81

Gifts 83

Gratitude 85

Grief / Grieving / Service 87

Guidance 89

Healing 91

Home 93

Hurt .... .95

Ideas 97

Jealousy 99

Kindness 101

Listening 103

Loneliness 105

Love 107

Marriage 109

My Magical Self 111

My Place 113

Opinions 115

Patience 117

Peace of Mind 119

Power / Strength 121

Prayer 123

Priorities 125

Protection 127

Relaxation 129

Release of Others 131

Resentment 133

Responsibility 135

Risk-Taking 137

Safety 139

Self Care 141

Self Realization 143

Songs to Sing 145

Trust 147

Unity 149

Vacation 151

Values 153

Weight 155

Wisdom 157

Work Relationship 159

World Peace 161

APPENDIX

Suggested Reading 165

About the Author 167

INTRODUCTION

If you have ever felt alone, paralyzed by fear, anxiety-ridden, overwhelmed, or thought you were going mad, this book is for you. Whoever you are, whatever your situation, YOU are the reason this book was born.

Because I grew up with people who abused and neglected me, I felt unloved in a healthy way, and absolutely unlovable. I frequently felt like a dirty rag heaped on a pile of unwanted rags.

When I was overcome with fear and self-doubt, I yearned for one person who could tell me what to do. I needed a mentor to help me move through tough times and show me the world through different eyes.

There was a tiny spark within that knew better and I created in detail a wonderful, imaginary family whom I pretended looked for me. They would take me away, punish my family, and we would live happily ever after.

That didn't happen, so at sixteen I ran away, which was a wonderfully, wise choice.

After years of avoiding the dragons and demons that dwelled within (old memories and feelings), I faced down most of those invisible monsters. Through emotional healing, spiritual work, prayer, and ministerial school, I found I could lean on something greater.

In times when I feel uneasy, I ask myself, "What do I need and where can I get it?" I step forward into action to fill those needs. I ask my friends to support me when I need support.

When we become aware of how we are feeling by monitoring our body and thoughts, we can avoid crisis thinking by identifying and shifting thoughts of worry, fear or confusion.

First steps look and feel hard, whether we are learning to walk, or getting unstuck. When that first step is taken, everything falls into place and life feels easier, yes?

Reading this book is the first step because your desire for change has already set into motion an energy that will assist you in getting unstuck. Knowing the hardest step is over, just follow step-by-step and notice how you will live with ease.

I want to walk you through your difficult times. Take my hand and we shall walk together.

SUGGESTED WAYS TO USE THE BOOK

Look in the Contents to find the subject that is calling for your attention. Turn to that page. Now comes the most important part – read with an open mind. Be open to the possibility of seeing and doing something differently. Remember, if what you've been doing so far hasn't worked, wouldn't it be wise to try something different? So, with an open mind, read that section and decide if you want to move through your problem. If you want to change, keep reading.

The AFFIRM section is a way to shift your thinking. For instance, if you wear glasses and take them off, everything looks unclear. The minute you put on your glasses you see clearly. The mind is the same. We think a "fuzzy" thought that keeps us stuck. To change that thought, we affirm a new thought (even if we don't quite believe it yet). An Affirmation is as powerful as turning on the motor of your car. We are stuck until we turn the ignition key.

The WHAT TO DO section moves you onto the playing field of life and takes you out of the spectator stands watching your life go by. If you want to change, try out what is suggested. The saying, "nothing changes if nothing changes" makes sense.

When the word "Spirit" is used, please substitute the word you feel most comfortable using. Some people prefer God, Jesus, Allah, Krishna, Higher Power, Great Spirit, etc. It refers to the essence within you that is greater than the part of you that doubts yourself. It is the everlastingness of you that is unchanging regardless of what your body looks like and it remains after you have gone.

So using this book is pretty straightforward. If you need help along the way, please contact me at
Revjudywinkler@gmail.com.

May this ease your journey in life and may you find comfort, peace and deep joy in your heart.

Love and Blessings,
Judy Winkler

ABUNDANCE

Over thirty years ago, I moved to a new city. As a single mom, I felt totally responsible for the welfare of my family. Six weeks of job hunting proved unsuccessful and I was broke. I was scared, ashamed, and believed I was a failure. I fell into a deep depression.

The crushing blow was that my daughter's 13th birthday was at hand. I didn't have money to buy her a gift. I felt so ashamed. I hid in my room silently crying instead of doing what might have made her birthday fun, even if I couldn't buy her a gift. Instead, I focused on what was missing rather than what we had. I failed to see a precious, healthy daughter, family pets, rich soil to grow a vegetable garden, freedom to be in a new city with grand opportunities, and a hopeful future.

Just three months earlier, I was totally blind for 6 weeks due to a viral infection in the retinal wall. Now my eyesight was restored and the world was filled with possibilities.

What we focus on is what we experience. Have you noticed when you are hungry, you suddenly see signs for restaurants, or when you are shopping for a certain car, everywhere you look, you see that particular make and model? The surest way to experience abundance is to focus in on what we have, instead of what we do not have.

Let's assume our basic needs are met, such as a home, food, and clothing. Feelings of lack come from comparing ourselves to others or the belief that we and/or our lives *should* look a certain way. If we didn't compare ourselves with others and had no belief about what we should or shouldn't have, we would be more accepting and appreciative for what we DO have. Gratitude reaps abundance.

AFFIRM:

I know Spirit is the source of all abundance. My abundance is in direct relationship to my understanding that all good comes from Spirit. There is enough. I open my eyes to accept my good.

Because Spirit is generous and always gives, I freely circulate all that I have. I make room for the new to come to me. I re-focus on what I have and give thanks for all I've been given.

WHAT TO DO

1. Balance your checkbook.

2. Create a budget based on absolute necessities.

3. Go through your closets, drawers and garage. Give away or sell what you don't use or need.

4. Thank Spirit for all you have.

5. Repeat the following statements each morning and evening:

   ❖ THERE IS ENOUGH
   ❖ I AM A GOOD STEWARD
   ❖ I AM WORTHY OF AN ABUNDANT LIFE
   ❖ MONEY FLOWS TO ME
   ❖ IT'S OKAY TO HAVE MORE THAN MY PARENTS

ACCEPTANCE

The deepest pain I've caused myself has been not accepting situations, conditions, or myself. I've always held an imaginary view of what I believed was expected. If I didn't measure up, I cursed myself, my circumstances and my life in general. I would say, "A woman in your situation *should* have more."

All the women I knew seemed to have more – a husband, a home, a new car, nice clothes, vacations, and I struggled to pay the rent. I definitely did **not** feel acceptance. However, the moment I turn to look within instead of what is around me, noticing what I **do** have, what I **can** give, how I **can** create, the energy shifts and the pain disappears.

It occurred to me that 24 hours of energy was given to me each day. I could use it to create and move forward or I could use the energy to complain, feel sorry for myself, or whine to an indulgent friend. I now choose to use the energy to accept where I am right this minute and know deep within me that this is the exact place I need to be in order to change. I begin right here to move ahead.

AFFIRM:

Today, I accept myself just as I am. I am exactly where I am supposed to be. Today, I will not compare my inside with the outside of anyone else. Likewise, I accept others as they are. All of us are doing our best at the moment.

If life were a play, Spirit is the director. We each have a part to play, which is valuable and important, even if it seems otherwise. In other words, our job is to be our best self in each moment. Spirit is responsible for the outcome. Accepting our role for today brings serenity. Resistance brings pain.

WHAT TO DO

1. Ask three friends to describe your assets.

2. Write them down.

3. Add your own assets to the list. Read it daily.

4. Affirm, "I accept the lessons I am learning from the circumstances of my life."

5. Thank Spirit for who you are right now. Ask for peace of mind with your *role* for today.

ACCIDENTS

Accidents are incidents, which surprise us and occur without our control. What if there were no accidents? What if each circumstance was really a plan, which includes greater good than we could imagine? Would that change your idea about circumstances?

For many years, I have made a practice that when I hear a siren of an emergency vehicle, or witness a roadside accident; I immediately send a prayer and blessings to everyone involved. I say, "Bless you. Be you comforted." Thoughts (prayers) manifest into form. Our word is very powerful.

A few years ago, I read a story that gave me chills. A freeway accident victim wrote it. He died at the scene and described himself hovering above his body, watching people scrambling to revive him. A passerby uttered a powerful prayer that moved him back into his body and he was revived. I wondered if this prayer came from my children, my students, or me who were taught to send prayers to those in need. We never know how powerful our prayers can be.

AFFIRM:

Today, even though there appear to be accidents, Spirit is in control and knows exactly what's happening. There are countless gifts that come from each situation. I open my heart to allow these gifts to be revealed.

WHAT TO DO

1. Look for the unexpected gifts you received from past events.

2. Tell people what they mean to you in the moment.

3. Ask Spirit to reveal what you need to know.

ADDICTION / ALCOHOLISM

I was married to an alcoholic and drug user. In fact, he had just come out of a recovery program when our paths crossed for the second time. He was going through a tough divorce. We talked by phone and I tried to fix him up with all my girlfriends but he wasn't interested. He seemed to thrive on our friendship. But that's another book.

At that time, I didn't realize I was a food addict and a workaholic. I was aware I was compulsive about order but in my arrogance I believed I simply had high standards. The point is that it is easy to identify addiction in others and label them, and ignore our own. I define addiction as a dependency or habit where we give away our power to something outside of the self. In other words, our addiction drives us instead of our higher thinking.

When I was suffering from food addiction, I would eat so much food at night, I could hardly move. Food anesthetized me so I felt no emotion. I cursed myself for eating so much, for being so fat. I would awaken the next morning with compulsive thoughts about what I would eat, where, and when. I struggled to get through my workday just so I could repeat the pattern one more time. I prayed no one would call because I'd rather eat and watch TV than talk with anyone. I gave all my power, my thoughts, and my desires to food. My food became my best friend. The TV was my companion and I hated myself for what I had become – unattractive, isolated, depressed.

In desperation I attended overeaters anonymous, had a wonderful sponsor who lovingly guided me through my changes. In turn, I became a sponsor to others. Although that was years ago, I still struggle with food issues, eating the wrong foods at the wrong times for the wrong reasons.

The difference today is that it is manageable. It is a temporary situation, not a way of life. I am healthy and I feel good about myself. I have a rich, full productive life. Addicts have no life. I was there, so I know.

AFFIRM:

Today, I turn my life and my will over to the care of my Higher Power, as I understand Him/Her. I am powerless over my addiction, which is a disease. Spirit, however, has all the power in the universe and can, if I am willing to surrender, keep me sober/clean/abstinent. Today is all there is, so just for today, I pray for help - and accept it. Every choice I make supports my recovery rather than my disease. I do whatever is necessary to recover.

WHAT TO DO

1. Find a 12-Step recovery group and attend meetings.

2. Get a sponsor right away.

3. Read the Big Book (Alcoholics Anonymous).

ADJUSTMENT
(*See* HARMONY)

It is never the situation; it is my unwillingness to adjust that causes me discomfort. The harder I try to make things look the way I expect them to, the more unhappy I become. I was taught never to settle for less than I expect. I interpreted that to mean that things better turn out the way I plan them or the world is going to be pretty sorry. I thought people who adapted to situations were weak and just gave up. Now I see it takes courage to be willing to yield, to adapt, and adjust to what is happening. Strong people can yield. Resistance <u>causes</u> a problem. "Thy will be done," or "oh well," are great phrases for a quick re-adjustment.

A friend told me that his company was moving 3,000 miles away. Although he was a highly paid engineer, he refused to move with the company and adjust. He stayed and couldn't find a job for 5 months. He sank into depression. Still he refused to reconsider the offer to move with his company. Finally, he called his old boss and said he'd move. He met and married his wife in the new state, started a family, and found the joy he had always yearned for.

One vacation we packed up our 5-year old and our dog into our camper van and headed out to explore some national forests. We were in Utah near Idaho. I remember winding down a mountain road. The intoxicating fragrance of apple blossoms breathed their essence into the van. I felt so connected to all of life. We turned a corner. Out of nowhere came the most magnificent scene I've ever witnessed. We stopped the van and got out. The sight was like an awesome painting and we were standing in the middle of it. The backdrop was the majestic purple snow-capped Rocky Mountains. Beneath the craggy peaks were rolling green meadowlands carpeted with yellow, white, and orange wildflowers. Beneath that was rich, brown soil that I could almost smell. All of that kissed the perimeter of Bear Lake – a vast crystal clear blue lake that sparkled like a huge jewel from heaven. I never expected that marvelous treat because it had been invisible to us.

Faith is to know that there is a bigger picture than we cannot yet see. Life is like driving on a mountain road and only Spirit knows there's a magical surprise waiting around the bend. Just because we cannot see it, doesn't mean it isn't there.

AFFIRM:

Today, I release my investment in the outcome of circumstances and adjust to what is. The faster I adjust, the happier I am.

WHAT TO DO

1. Write down what you believe you will lose if you yield or surrender to the outcome or a situation.

2. Write down your fears on a piece of paper and put it in an envelope addressed to God. Release it.

3. Picture yourself adjusting and yielding to the change – how does it feel?

AGE

Ever notice that we are youthful and beautiful in our dreams? If spirit sees us this way, we need to see ourselves this way too. When our hearts are open to take in new experiences, we feel youthful and energetic. When we are willing to laugh and play, we feel young. Children are admonished to "act your age," which means be like old fuddy-duddies. Now that I qualify to be an old fuddy-duddy, I hope I never act my age. I love to do childlike things. I love to explore and take in new information. I believe I'll always be ageless because so many things fascinate me. The health practice of excellent nutrition, rest, and exercise keep us young and alive.

A friend shared that as she ages, she feels closer to her peers because they share the common leveling experience of being closer to the end of this lifetime.

AFFIRM:

Today, I know that there is no time in the spiritual dimension. My age is based on how I look at life and how willing I am to participate in life. Age is neither good nor bad. Young is not better than old. Age is simply our belief about it and our reaction to it. I know that years have given me enlightenment and wisdom, which provide me with more gifts to share.

WHAT TO DO

1. What do you believe about aging?

2. Finish this sentence: I want to remain young because . . .

3. Ask Spirit to reveal how your experience and wisdom can be used.

AGREEMENT
(*See* HARMONY)

Have you ever noticed that when you are very comfortable with what you really believe the less you need to voice those beliefs? In fact, the more we are comfortable about what we stand for, the less we need anyone to agree with us. Our lives show what we believe and nothing needs to be said.

As an example, I believe that if we notice that something needs attention, instead of getting upset, we can fix it. An outside neighborhood taco shop always had filthy tables and benches. As I waited for my food, I said to myself, "Somebody needs to clean up this mess." I realized I was somebody so I asked for a damp cloth to wipe the tables and benches. A friend drove by. She thought I worked at the taco stand because she couldn't believe I would offer to clean the tables for nothing. Now whenever I go there, they prepare a warm cloth for me to clean off the tables and benches. I'm not ashamed to be seen doing what appears to be a custodial task. I'm grateful I can make one area of the community clean and appealing to others. In other words, my actions are in agreement with what I stand for.

AFFIRM:

I am in harmony with the Spirit that dwells within. My choices are in accordance with my inner values and ethics. I know what is right for me. I am clear about who I am and what I stand for. What others think of me has nothing to do with me. No one need agree with me nor I with him or her. I stand in my truth. If I decide I need to speak up, it is to voice my truth, not to coerce or manipulate.

WHAT TO DO

1. Turn to the pages on Values (page 153) and do the exercise listed.

2. In your family of origin what did you learn about standing in your truth?

3. Is that true for you today? Live what you believe.

ANGER / ANTAGONISM

When I was in middle school, our class debated the pros and cons of religion. I argued against the concept of God, religion, and The Bible. I argued well, reducing my opponent, Shirley, to tears. Shirley, a devoutly religious person argued for her life; I was just toying with her mind. Inside I had struggled with all the questions and answers. The only ingredient I never considered was heart. I didn't feel what it would be like to have something so dear to the heart be destroyed publicly. Although I won the debate, I felt unpopular with the class and myself.

I do not argue anymore. What I see outside myself is a reflection of what is going on within me. No one needs to see things my way and I am open to take in what I choose. No one can make me believe any other way without my consent. Mitch Albom wrote, "Love or die" in his book, "Tuesdays with Morrie."

AFFIRM:

Today, I allow the love of Spirit to fill my heart so all I feel and see is love. Love is in me and around me, moving through me. Love dwells in all people. Today, I choose to see the Divine love in each and every person I meet. I silently say hello to all humankind and bless them.

WHAT TO DO

1. To get antagonistic feelings out safely, find a private place. Fold a clean washcloth in half. Place 1" or 2" of the fold in your front teeth and clench down. (This muffles sounds so no one will hear you.)

2. Now scream and shout angry words. Say, "I release all anger."

3. When finished, take 3 deep breaths and re-read the affirmation above.

4. Breathe into the areas of the body that still hold tension.

ANSWERS

Most of life has felt so frightening to me that I thought if I had answers, I would be prepared to protect myself. So I gathered as much information as I could to stay in control. When answers came to me, I questioned and doubted each one because I was so terrified of being wrong or making a fool of myself. I was heavily invested in keeping up the masquerade of looking perfect in every way. It is difficult to take in new information and appear perfect at the same time.

Often answers came to me intuitively. I pushed them away, or tried to figure out the consequences of each possible action or direction. As I began to trust life more, when answers came to me, I sifted them through a mental checklist. I asked myself if the answer was loving, kind, and for the highest good of all. I also noticed that if I felt pressured to take action right away, as though this is my last chance in life, I knew this is not the wisest answer.

The greatest peace of all comes from knowing we can always re-choose so there is no wrong answer.

AFFIRM:

Today, I ask for help. Spirit has the answers. I find them within so I am open to receive the good that is there for me. I pray, meditate, read, and call those people who support me. Wherever I turn, I get my answers. I am well cared for today.

WHAT TO DO

1. Identify what you need.

2. Where can you get it?

3. Stretch and ask for help. It is perfectly ok to do so.

4. Put a pad of paper by your bed. Answers frequently come at night through dreams.

5. Watch for answers. They may be very different from YOUR expectations.

ANXIETY

Anxiety could have been my middle name. It described me perfectly. I never felt at peace about anything or anyone. I worried about what might happen, what might not happen, or what did happen. You can imagine that all that worrying kept me from being present in my own body in the moment.

During one of my all-night worry marathons, I asked myself, what do I need to let go of in order to have peace of mind? The thought that I would need to surrender something scared me. That night, I pictured myself being held in the loving wings of an angel who enfolded me and protected me from harm. I saw myself being rocked and soothed. This visual has been a constant comfort to me. I felt as though I surrendered into loving arms.

AFFIRM:

Today, I breathe deeply. As I feel my heartbeat, I hear the voice of Spirit saying, "All is well - all is well - all is well - all is well." I rest in Spirit's loving arms. I allow the peace of Spirit to fill my very soul. Spirit is my protector; my guide and my great comforter. I have nothing to fear. "All is well. All is well. I feel at peace."

WHAT TO DO

1. Remember a time in your life when you felt safe and secure.

2. Imagine you are in that time right now. Visualize with all its color, sounds, and fragrances. Feel every feeling. Linger until you feel at peace.

3. Know you can return to that place of peace any time you wish. It is only a thought away.

BALANCE

Have you ever noticed that discontent is nature's way of indicating that we are out of balance? It is simply a request to re-align.

A private pilot I used to fly with explained to me that the auto pilot device could only work by moving off its course. In other words, to be brought back on course, we must first move away. So feeling out of balance is the best way to recognize a correction needs to be made. Isn't that great?

AFFIRM:

Today, I re-align myself. Spirit has a built-in balancing device called discontent. Our perfect body-machine brings itself back into balance by getting our attention. I listen to the signals, subtle at first, then stronger and stronger. I mentally look at each aspect of my life to evaluate what needs attention.

WHAT TO DO

1. Ask yourself, how am I doing spiritually? Pray, meditate, read and listen to inspirational messages.

2. Ask yourself, how am I doing physically? Eat food that provides the highest energy. Rest, exercise, and take a warm bath.

3. Ask how am I doing emotionally? Evaluate social relationships, family, recreation, and occupation.

BEAUTY

Recently an old family picture came to me. It was taken when I was 16. Even though I wore no make-up, I was beautiful enough to be a movie star. I looked like Elizabeth Taylor. It saddened me to realize that I never recognized or acknowledged my beauty. Now, as a grandmother, I believe I'm beautiful. Our perception is what makes the difference.

In one culture we would be considered a treasured beauty; in another, we wouldn't measure up. I ask you, "By whose standards do you accept or reject yourself?"

AFFIRM:

Today, I surround myself with beauty. Beauty is reflected from the inside out. Beauty is at the core of who I am. Spirit's love shines through me. It draws people to me. My presence blesses and heals everyone I meet. What is more beautiful than Spirit's creation - flowers, trees, sunrises, mountains, and oceans? It is all for us to appreciate.

WHAT TO DO

1. If your body could bless and heal all people each time they looked at you, how would you see yourself?

2. Find a flower and study it carefully. Notice its beauty. How are you like the flower?

3. Surround yourself with beauty. Go to an art gallery or plant nursery or listen to your favorite music.

4. Ask what does my living space say about me? Clean up clutter, make it inviting and let it express you.

BEING ME
(*See* VALUES)

During a meditation I had a vision that changed the way I view life. I saw myself about to enter the Holland Tunnel in N.Y., (an underground tunnel lined with white tiles).

The tunnel had my name over the entrance. As I walked into my tunnel, the walls became mosaics depicting my life up to that point. Each time I moved, the pictures changed. Each tunnel entrance had other people's names over them.

This meditation was a profound shift in the way saw life. It dispels comparison and competition. My life experience is a creation made by my own thoughts – which can be changed at any point along the way.

AFFIRM:

Today, I honor myself. My path has my name on it and only I can walk this path. No one can do it for me, nor can I walk anyone else's path. Spirit guides each step so I feel safe.

WHAT TO DO

1. Ask Spirit to reveal who you are and what is your path.

2. Notice when your eyes are on other people's paths.

3. Look at the section on Values (page 153) and do the exercise.

BLAME

I blamed my family, my circumstances, and everyone around me for my difficulties. I had problems at home in a dysfunctional family. I had problems at school due to dyslexia, language, speaking, reading, emotional trauma and self-consciousness. I played my life as though I was a victim and the sweet heroine in my story and everyone else was a bad guy. When I awakened to the game I was playing, I took back the responsibility and I know that whatever happens, happens. Blame keeps me from correcting the situation and keeps me glued to the past. I can see what is required of me and do it.

Neale Donald Walsh told a story, which I'll attempt to paraphrase. It was about little angels who were bright twinkling lights. God asked who was willing to be darkness so others could shine more brightly (by contrast). One angel volunteered. He likened this to our unhappy childhood. That our parents, siblings, or whomever caused us the greatest pain were really angels who loved us so much, they were willing to come to earth in darkness to give us the experiences we needed to allow us to shine more brilliantly.

Blame limits us from living life full out. Blame brings shame and shame is slow death.

AFFIRM:

Today, I let go of blame. Spirit holds no blame, and I am made in God's image. I forgive myself for past mistakes and I forgive others.

WHAT TO DO

1. Take responsibility for your actions. Admit when you are wrong. Apologize, make amends, forget it, and move on.

2. Dissolve the need to blame yourself or others.

3. Stay in the present moment.

4. Ask yourself, "What valuable lesson or gift came from this experience?"

BURDENS / STRESS

Burdens and stress come when we believe that we need to be different from who and what we are. My life has been spent proving to the world that I was Super-Judy, able to leap tall buildings in a single bound. I felt responsible for everything. My blanket solution was to work harder and faster. I thought I could handle anything if I just made more of an effort. I was a wife, a mother, a full time employee, went to school, volunteered, was politically active, kept up social obligations, sewed all the clothes for the family, baked my own bread and wondered why I got tired. My investment was looking good to everyone else as well as myself.

Feeling burdened is Spirit's way of showing us we carry more than is necessary. I used to believe that if I am a spiritual person, I must be a martyr. A woman once told me, "Get off the cross, Judy, we need the wood." A sign above my desk says, "Good morning, Judy, this is God. I won't be needing your help today."

AFFIRM:

Today, I listen to each sign that tells me I'm taking on more than is necessary. I am a silent witness who stands at the doorway of my mind and body, asking, "Who am I trying to impress?"

Today I give to Spirit all that I cannot handle. Today, I am comfortable with who I am and how I express myself. I just show up and do my best. My best is good enough.

WHAT TO DO

1. Notice when you take on too much.

2. Who are you trying to impress? You don't get extra points for carrying more.

3. What clues can you watch for to identify when you are over-burdened?

4. Write down 3 things that you can do when you feel stressed or burdened, such as go for a walk, meditate, etc. Put your list in a highly visible place so you have an action plan.

5. Prioritize and just do the most important things. Less is more if done with love.

6. Give Spirit everything you cannot do anything about.

BUSINESS

Through the years, I've had a number of occupations, positions, and participated in volunteer projects. One career I had was being a minister and heading up a church. I couldn't support the church and the church couldn't sustain itself or me, so when I hit a debt of $10,000.00, I felt out of integrity to owe so much money without a way to repay the debt, so I quit. I felt as if I was divorcing a whole congregation. I was emotionally crushed by my sense of failure.

I registered with a temporary agency just to get some income flowing. It occurred to me then that I have always been a temporary employee for God. I am put in different places at different times to do certain jobs and touch certain lives, and nothing is permanent—even if I work for many years in the same job.

Would you feel differently about your job if you saw yourself as a temporary employee, on a temporary assignment to go in, do your best, touch as many lives as possible, and move on when something else calls you?

AFFIRM:

Today, I work for God. God is my employer, and the president of the board of my directors. My actions are from the highest point of view and my choices are for the highest good of all. Every task I perform, I perform for God. My vocation is only one avenue of my good. My gifts and talents are demonstrated wherever I go, whatever I do. Everything I think, say, and do blesses and heals the planet.

WHAT TO DO

1. Are you doing Spirit's work? What might that be?

2. Ask your close friends where they see you doing your work to celebrate Spirit.

3. Ask Spirit what you need to be doing right now.

CHEERFULNESS

The silly, the funny, and the absurd are all Spirit's toys to lighten the world. Today, I let joy flow from my heart and I feel wonderful!

Cheerfulness is a conscious choice. We can celebrate in joy with each breath or we can curse all that comes our way. We decide. When we laugh, we feel better, and when we criticize, we feel worse.

Think of the people you enjoy being around—are they criticizers or cheerful ones? Smile and the world DOES smile with you.

AFFIRM:

Today, I choose to be cheerful. Each smile is a silent message from Spirit. Without words, my smile says, "The Spirit in me embraces the Spirit in you." My joy is powerful for it keeps Spirit-like thoughts flowing.

WHAT TO DO

1.   Smile all day long.

2.   Laugh out loud as often as you can.

3.   Get a joke book from the library.

4.   Make funny faces.

5.   Rent a comedy video.

CHILDREN

I was a most reliable baby sitter and parents could depend on me, but I never felt kids really liked me. I still feel starched around little kids, anticipating they will cry or reject me.

It amazes me to see how beautifully each of my own children interacts with kids. They are like Pied Pipers because all kids love them.

Before I had children, my favorite cousin, Frankie, asked me to baby sit the youngest of her three children, a boy who was three years old. She and her friend, Daisy, the mother of five needed to be away for the day. They returned before dinnertime. He was a dear little boy and seemed very happy to spend the day with my animals and me. He talked non-stop the entire day. The women asked me how things went. I said he seemed just fine but I wondered with all their other children, how could they listen to a child all day long. They answered, in unison, "Who listens?" At that time, I thought it was so unloving to think that a mother didn't listen to her children. Now, their response makes me laugh.

I think that children are sent to us so we can see what is unhealed in ourselves. As a child, I wasn't permitted to cry, make noise, or speak up, so I was annoyed when my children cried, made noise, or talked back. Children do cry, make noise and voice their opinions. We'd be foolish to think otherwise.

My oldest daughter had colic and cried for 3 months. I felt like crying myself for 3 months. Each time she cried, it was like calling up that inner howl that I'd buried from my own childhood. All my years of suppressed cries seemed to come out through her. I could hardly stand it.

Little seemed to comfort her. I rocked her, walked her, bounced her, gave her warm baths, drove her around in the car, played music, and patted her. Nothing helped. When it was discovered she was allergic to milk and we put her on goat's milk, the crying stopped and my sanity was restored. I learned that I had unshed tears.

What are your children teaching you about yourself? What gifts can you give them? How can you help them express?

AFFIRM:

Today, I honor the children. I honor my inner child by hearing her/his deepest wants and needs. My playfulness has places and times to express. My clothes and living space express my child part in special ways. I take risks. I feel safe to express the child within me. I let myself be close to others.

WHAT TO DO

1. Find your favorite picture of yourself when you were a small child.

2. Imagine yourself nurturing that child. Ask it what it needs and wants and provide it. Keep your word.

3. Notice how children play with each other. Can you incorporate their loving, forgiving, honest, expressive qualities?

4. Ask Spirit to show you how to be a child again.

CLAIMING MY PLACE
(*See* BEING ME, CONFIDENCE)

My favorite friends on the block wore uniforms and attended the neighborhood grammar school, St. Joan of Arc. I sneaked into the church that was attached to the school as often as possible. I wanted to be Catholic. I wanted to wear a uniform instead of hand-me-downs. I wanted to belong to a group so I could fit in instead of standing out as an odd duck. I wanted to be popular. In college I lived in a sorority house for a summer at UCLA. I wanted to belong so I pretended I was a Sigma Kappa, or whatever it was called. Being me wasn't good enough, I thought.

As I write, I search for words to drape you in self-contentment so you know being yourself is exactly what is required to claim your place. Know that the more you dare to reveal yourself to the world, the more you are at home. In other words, belonging or claiming your place becomes unimportant because being yourself brings you to a level of participation in life where you play your position on the court. There is a huge difference between being in the spectator stands as an observer and being out there on the court, being yourself and playing the game of life.

During personal coaching session, many clients confide, "I don't belong, I don't fit in, I can't find my niche."

We need to know we are here by design. Just as a jigsaw puzzle needs every single piece to bring the picture into form; we are an important piece in life's puzzle. Each one of us has a special place, a special job, and a gift to give.

AFFIRM:

Today, I feel loved and accepted. My work is valuable and I'm doing a fine job. I am requested, respected, and highly rewarded. The world has a special place for me. I am wanted and needed, and no one can give my special gift as I can. The world is waiting for me with open arms, and I step into it with ease.

WHAT TO DO

1. Identify your special gifts.

2. One way to identify your gift is this exercise. Number thirty separate pages in a writing tablet. Put it beside your bed.

3. When you awaken each morning (for thirty consecutive days), write the answer to this question:

If money were no object and I didn't have to go to work today, this is what I'd do: Write as fast as you can without editing, judging, or criticizing. It's okay if you write down all the jobs you've put off doing around the house. Do NOT read what you have written. Just turn the page over.

4. At the end of thirty days read all the pages. You will find a common thread that appears.

5. Without revealing what you discovered, ask a friend to find the thread, or gift.

CONFIDENCE
(See BEING ME, COURAGE)

Lack of confidence appears when I think I need to be different from who I am. I've lived most of my life as a shy, private person who does not like to be the center of attention. Even though I've given hundreds of talks, when I'm asked to speak publicly I get nervous and feel for a moment that I lack confidence because I have a vision of what a public speaker should look like and act like.

I was at a party with a good friend. When I was spontaneously called on to do an invocation in front of many people, I just did it without any hesitation. My friend knows I'm shy so he commented how well I stepped up to the plate when called on. I explained that something very different happens when I am called to give service, such as lead a group or share information because I am needed. This duality puzzled me until I saw the correlation between the thought that I need to be different from who I am. Being who I am is just what was requested. The expectation that I need to be like someone else is slow death because it keeps me from expressing at the highest level.

AFFIRM:

Today, I stand firmly in the truth that I am fine the way I am. I am Spirit's expression of me, being me today. I have been created by a loving presence that has bestowed gifts and talents on me. I know my value and bring it to the world with confidence and ease. My confidence is increased each time I step through a barrier and take a risk.

WHAT TO DO

1. List your fears - large and small.

2. Considering your style do you dive into cold water, or inch your way in? Decide on the fear you wish to move through.

3. Decide whom you wish to join you, if anyone.

4. Commit your plan to another person along with the time that you will perform it. For example, you fear going to new places and doing new things so you decide to attend a dance this week. Perhaps you ask a friend to join you, and you agree to stay for 20 minutes no matter how scared you feel.

5. Even though we know Spirit is always with us, when we get scared, we forget. Use this mantra: "Thank you God for being with me. Thank you God for being with me. Thank you God for being with me."

CONFUSION
(*See* SAFETY)

When I was a small child, my father occasionally took us out to buy ice cream. He would ask what flavor I wanted. Because he was impatient and unpredictable, when he asked what flavor I wanted, I had to answer immediately or I'd get none. If I chose a flavor I didn't like, I had to eat it anyway without complaints.

The consequences attached to decision-making, as a child felt heavy and often grim. As a result, I either made no decision and braced myself for life's consequential disappointments, or snatched at any decision just to get it out of the way.

Claiming confusion was one way I avoided making decisions, however I felt stuck and extremely unhappy.

Fortunately, now I am able to take the time I need to make a decision and I truly enjoy my many preferences.

AFFIRM:

Spirit and I stand together. We make a great team.

WHAT TO DO

1. Act as if there are NO mistakes. From now on every choice is the perfect one for now.

2. Ask yourself, "If I DID decide, what would happen? What might be the consequences?"

3. If you don't like your first decision, re-choose. If you don't like that one, re-choose. It is just fine to re-choose and take action now.

COURAGE
(*See* BEING ME, CONFIDENCE)

When I was 60, a friend and neighbor locked herself out of her house. Her unit was two stories above ground level. She came to me for help. I borrowed a ladder, put it against her outside balcony and climbed up, climbed over her balcony wall, walked through her house and let her in her front door. I was performing a service so I didn't fear the height nor think of limitations. I only saw the need to get her into her home without damaging locks, screens, etc. My agility and quick thinking amazed her. I simply forgot my age and possible danger.

Someone asked me where I get the courage to face inner demons and walk through "the dark night of the soul." My comment was, if I don't face down my fear, it will run my life. I remind myself that God didn't bring me through all of life's experiences to drop me on my behind.

AFFIRM:

Today, I have all the courage I need. Spirit provides all the strength I need to move through each experience. I stretch and grow. No thing can harm me because Spirit is for me and with me. With God, I can handle anything.

WHAT TO DO

1. If you *were* courageous, what would your life look like?

2. What do you need to release in order to move forward?

3. What small step can you take today to confront your fear?

4. Who is your model for courage? Ask him or her for advice.

CRITICISM

My arrogance led me to think that I knew better than anyone so I made it my job to critique everyone and everything. I constantly criticized. The majority of it was done on the inside and came out with commentaries, particularly about someone's wardrobe, makeup, or behavior.

It truly did not occur to me that people are different. I believed there was only one way to do things and it was **my** way. I found it much easier to criticize than live my own life fully.

When attending a class, I silently critiqued the instructor and constructed more effective ways I would present the material. My call was to teach and share at a higher level, so instead of taking action myself, I criticized what I saw.

Criticism is an inner call to take action or deliver communication.

When a critical voice begins in your mind, imagine you are alone in a mountain cabin. You hear a wild animal at the door. Would you invite it in to run wild or would you slam the door? Slam the door! When you think critical thoughts, slam the door. Then ask what action do I need to take or what communication do I need to deliver?

AFFIRM:

Today, there is nothing in me that needs to be criticized nor condemned. Everyone is an expression of Spirit therefore there is no thing to criticize. My purpose is to bless and heal the planet, so everything I think, say, and do supports this intent.

WHAT TO DO

1. Identify the critical/negative thought. An example might be "I can't write a book."

2. Identify the feeling. An example might be, "I'm mad at myself for not writing."

3. Go deeper within to uncover the core belief. An example might be, "I've got nothing worth saying so I'm worthless."

4. Choose an alternative thought from critical/negative to accepting/positive. An example might be, "I have valuable ideas to share."

5. Choose an alternate behavior such as, call a friend who will validate your feelings, write out some ideas to share.

6. Notice how critical/negative feelings then change to peaceful, serene feelings.

DEATH

A sure way to lessen the pain of separation is to continually let those around you know how precious they are to you. We pay insurance premiums so we have peace of mind; letting others know what they mean to you will give you peace of mind when they die.

I ran away from home at 16 and never returned. I felt unprotected and betrayed by my mother because of major incidents. When I was 2 ½ my father, who was a stranger to me, took me to a new state to set up a home and wait for my mother and brother. I felt she threw me away and that she knew how painful the experience would be without her. With an abusive father and brother, she didn't protect me, and when I asked for her intervention to stop the sexual abuse, she didn't believe me. I gave up on her completely at age 10.

My mother died before I matured enough to reconcile with her. The pain of her death cut deeply into me and my deepest regret is that I know I would have loved her as a person, under different circumstances.

AFFIRM:

Today, I know there is no death in the mind of Spirit. Death is stepping from one dimension to another. The essence of who we are does not change. Outer form may change, but life is everlasting. If I moved to another part of our continent, my love would not diminish. Why would it change if I or someone else moved to the next dimension?

Each day, I tell those around me how precious they are to me so I'm certain there is no unfinished business should this be our last encounter.

WHAT TO DO

1. If someone you know is dying, ask him or her what they need from you. Perhaps they just need to talk, or want help with their fears of what to expect on the other side. Perhaps they want forgiveness, or prayers, or errands, or talking with family members. Decide if you are able to provide it and say so. Also, tell that person what you want from them and ask if they agree to provide it.

2. If you are dying, determine what you need and ask the people who can best provide it. Ask them if they are willing to give you what you need. If not, find someone who can. Be sure to ask what they need from you. Decide if you are willing to do it and then tell them.

3. Make each encounter the quality of a final encounter. Leave each person with the thoughts and words they can cherish if this were your last encounter.

DEBT
(See ABUNDANCE)

Debt has changed my life. I left the pulpit because I felt out of integrity owing $10,000 and not knowing how to pay it back. I paid back my debt within a year and turned my situation around.

Parenthetically, when I left the ministry (if ministers ever really do leave), I began to find God.

At one time, my liquid assets were $6.00. My choice was to put gasoline in the car or buy food. A few times in my life, I have been concerned that I might be homeless. I voiced my fear to a cousin who assured me that I could always live with him. So knowing that, I felt I had a safety net if things got worse. Even though it would have been fun to live with this cousin, alas, things got better.

AFFIRM:

Today, I am watchful over the small things, so the big things take care of themselves. I am a good steward. I buy only what I can afford. I make wise choices. I have no need to impress anyone. Spirit has given me wisdom. I save, I tithe, I share, and spend.

WHAT TO DO

1. Look at your stuff. If you separated the stuff you needed from the stuff you wanted, which items would go? Let go of stuff.
2. Before you buy something, ask yourself if you <u>need</u> it. If your answer is, "I want it," ask why. (If we think stuff will bring happiness, we are not at peace inside.)

3. Before you buy something, ask yourself if you have the ready cash to pay for it. If your answer is no, save your money to buy it.

4. Ask advice from someone whose finances are in order.

DEPRESSION

Feelings that are pressed down or unexpressed lead to depression. I spent years in depression. I was very angry with myself for not being perfect all the time and for imagined foolish mistakes. I was angry with the people from my past that hurt me, angry at circumstances, and angry with people around me who took advantage of me.

At that time, I didn't have ways to protect myself from being influenced or overpowered by others. Because I wasn't shown how to deal with anger, I turned the anger inward and shoved it down along with all the other feelings I hid inside. I didn't even know it was okay to ask for help. I wasted precious time away from my family and friends because I'd lock myself in my room and feel sorry for myself.

Now, and again I may feel blue, but it doesn't last long and I can ride it through by letting out my feelings and sharing them with others.

AFFIRM:

Today, Spirit that dwells within knows what I need to take care of myself. This is a safe world, and it is okay for me to let my feelings out. Today, I write out exactly what is bothering me including any feelings I have bottled inside. I am led to the perfect people who will support me through this. It is okay to ask for help.

WHAT TO DO

1. Write out how you feel.

2. Draw/scribble a picture that shows how you feel.

3. Fold a washcloth in half. Place the center of the fold an inch or two in your front teeth. Clench your teeth and yell what feelings you've written or drawn. No one will hear you if you use a washcloth this way.

4. Ask for help. It is okay to do so.

ECONOMIC SECURITY
(*See* ABUNDANCE, DEBT)

One evening I pondered what I might say and do if the Lord came to me and said, "Judy, follow me." I pictured my response, "Wait a second, I've got to pay the mortgage, get my Visa card and curling iron." I laughed at myself, and saw where I had placed my security. I can't be spiritual when I'm fretting about upcoming bills, and how I look. Yet I can't be free to earn and pay my bills if I don't put my faith in Spirit first.

I've had roller coaster experiences with finances. I've had more than I knew what to do with and I've had close to nothing and was a breath away from being on the street. I've felt richer in times of economic poverty and poorer in times when money came so fast, that I forgot to deposit checks.

AFFIRM:

Today, I know that Spirit provides for me. My needs are already met. I will always have enough money, food, clothes, so I have total peace of mind.

WHAT TO DO

1. Ask what *is* necessary for you to feel secure.

2. Decide what steps you can take to help you feel more secure.

3. Ask people who you think have economic security how they achieved it.

4. Read *The Richest Man in Babylon.*

EMPLOYMENT
(*See* GIFTS, WORK)

Statistics indicate most people are dissatisfied with their work. I do **not** believe we were created to go to an unsatisfying job. I believe we were created to give our particular gift to the world, and in return, are well rewarded. In order to identify what our special gift is, we must stop long enough to look at our talents, our values, and our passions.

I've had many occupations. I've been a live-in maid, a waitress, a ski instructor, a radio operator for LAPD, a medical secretary, an assistant to a medical director, a fiscal control coordinator, a purchasing agent, a minister, a teacher, and a spiritual coach, to name a few jobs. Some were very lucrative, some were below minimum wage. Some I felt called to do, some were a means to an end. Each one was a gift. I made life long friends, had exciting adventures, and gained information. I learned about abilities, my weaknesses and myself.

There is profound truth in the Buddhist story of enlightenment. A monk states that before he was enlightened, he chopped wood and carried water. When he became enlightened, he chopped wood and carried water. In other words, we can perform the same tasks, but when we do so for the glory of a higher power, everything changes.

AFFIRM:

Today, I give my very best to my job. Whatever job I perform, it has value and meaning. My gifts are being revealed to me right now. I am open to receive. I refine my gifts so I give back into life at the highest level possible.

WHAT TO DO

1. If your circle of friends constituted a tribe and each person's name described how he or she behaved, what would your name be? Does that give you an idea of your gift?

2. What is it that you would drop everything to do? (For me, if someone requests spiritual coaching, I drop everything.)

3. What would you do for nothing? Where can you give your gift?

4. Ask friends what your gifts are.

5. Look at Values (page 153) and do the exercise.

ENLIGHTENMENT

The truth is, we are always filled with light. The wisdom of the ages dwells within us. We simply forget. Remembering who and what we are seems to be the key that brings us back into balance. Specifically, I give my spiritual muscles a workout by practicing being aware of the presence of the Divine within and around me. Just like going to the gym to strengthen our physical muscles, we can strengthen our spiritual muscles by performing spiritual practices such as meditating, chanting, artistic expression, being in nature, listening to music, whatever it is you can do to feel your connection to something greater.

Children may link church and spiritual enlightenment. However, going to church doesn't make one Christian any more than going to a garage makes one a car. The light is always within and the degree to which we experience this inner presence is exacted in measure on the outside by the life we lead.

I've been told that my voice and my presence bring peace and comfort. People tell me that just thinking of me brings them comfort and balance. I know it is the light within that lights the way for others.

Each of us has a brilliant light to shine outward into the world. Let your light shine!

AFFIRM:

Today, I let the light of Spirit that dwells within me shine forth. I look at all things from the highest point of view. I look for the good, the fine, the life enhancing, and the loving. I think on those things that are good and pure.

Today, I look for and see the good in everyone and everything - starting with myself.

WHAT TO DO

1. Create a sacred place, a corner of a room in your home that is your place of worship, pray, or meditate

2. Fill it with objects, pictures, and fragrances that saturate you with a deep sense of oneness with your Spirit.

4. Spend morning and evening time in that sacred place.

5. Ask Spirit what you need to know about your spiritual practice.

ENTHUSIASM

The root of the word enthusiasm comes from the Greek "to be possessed or inspired by a Spirit." I attended a forum given by Landmark Education, which gave me back my enthusiasm. Before the forum, my life felt gray, flat, and self-contained. The forum experience freed me to allow the passion to flow again.

I remember as a child, weeping when I heard a Thanksgiving song, "Come Ye Thankful People Come." It expresses gratitude for what is given while the music stirs hope for the future. I remember feeling a tingle up my spine when I sang the Star Spangled Banner. I remember being on a farm at 5 years old and knowing I was part of every living thing around me. I was filled with Spirit. Then, everything mattered.

As I grew older and a sense of helplessness and hopelessness pervaded, nothing mattered any more. I just got by. When I fell in love, my beloved mattered; when I became a mother, everything mattered, when my beloved left, nothing mattered. People influenced my state of mind. It got to a point where all I felt was disappointment and separation and sadness. Life became flat – without any feelings. I walked around dead inside my body. Does that sound familiar?

I ask you, what activities enthrall you so you forget to eat or sleep? What are you passionate about? Where do you suppose enthusiasm comes from?

AFFIRM:

Today, I permit my passion to come to the surface. It is okay to demonstrate enthusiasm. I allow the spark that is ignited by Spirit within to set me on fire. I listen and follow. My enthusiasm energizes others and me.

WHAT TO DO

1. Look at Values (page 153), to see which ones sets you on fire.

2. Decide to actively participate in something you believe in.

3. Daily, document what you've done to support what you believe in.

4. Ask Spirit to remove all blocks that keep your enthusiasm from bubbling up.

ENVY
(*See* JEALOUSY)

Can you believe that envy has nothing to do with the other person? It is a signal that something in you is yet to be fulfilled. Envy is a great gift to remind us that we are NOT doing what we are meant to do and we are not being who we are meant to be. If we envy another, it is an inner urge to get about our Father's business. What is it that your soul is calling you to do?

I envied dancers, singers, actors, but have been too shy to pursue a theatrical career. I took two acting classes in comedy improvisation that satisfied my performing urge. I am a ballroom dancer and I compose music and sing which satisfies my musical and dancing desires. Even though I don't perform publicly, my needs are met.

AFFIRM:

Today, each task is done with deliberate care. This is my way to celebrate my love for life. My focus is on quality. Everything I do, I do to express all that I am.

WHAT TO DO

1. Identify what is it that your soul is calling YOU to do.

2. Write down your unfulfilled dreams.

3. Which ones need your attention?

4. Ask Spirit to direct your path and lead you to the people who can support you in achieving your goals.

EXPECTATION

Many of my deepest disappointments in life have come from my expectations of others, but most of them have come from disappointments in myself. Whenever I don't keep an agreement with myself, I'm disappointed. When things don't out-picture as I planned, I am upset. I've held a deep belief that marriage is forever, jobs last 30 years, health should not decline, well maintained cars should last forever, etc.

Most expectations are not agreements – they are expected outcomes because we have held a picture of what we think things should look like. I'm sorry that my marriage didn't last forever, but I'm grateful to be free to experience life as I now do.

AFFIRM:

Today, I let go of any expectation or outcome to situations. A Divine Plan is working for my highest good. I do the footwork; Spirit handles the rest, including the results.

WHAT TO DO

1. Release control of the outcome of situations.

2. Read, *Love is Letting Go of Fear* by Gerald Jampolsky, M.D.

3. Imagine that your life is a screenplay in process. Different writers offer different endings. Each ending has positive results.

4. Relax and know that the perfect outcome is already in mind and that you will receive great gifts from it.

EYES

If you were blind for six weeks, do you think you would ever forget that experience? I forgot until my niece reminded me that she visited me during my bout with blindness. The irony is that all my life I've heard, "What beautiful eyes you have." My thought was, thank God they work so well and I can see things many people can't see. During my blindness, I recognized that what one sees has nothing to do with sight. I saw beyond the visible and understood beneath the seen.

The gripping thought that I couldn't support my family devastated me. Failing as a provider plagued me. I was haunted by this concern. What I experienced is that life has little to do with physical vision. I managed fine without sight. I cooked and cleaned, and my boss had a driver pick me up for work. I could answer the phone, record messages and dictate correspondence.

The doctors could not explain my sudden blindness except that a virus had gotten into the retinal wall area and they did not know what the outcome would be. I lived in darkness and the unknown for six weeks. Then one morning, I saw the shadow of my bedroom window. I felt hopeful. The next day I had enough vision to read the headlines of the newspaper if my nose was on the page. On the third day my sight returned completely. I was so relieved! I wrote, "When I was blind, I could see. Now that I can see, I'm blind." What a paradox!

AFFIRM:

Today, I see what I need to see. I look through eyes of love, so that which is revealed to me is a gift. I see from the highest point of view so I look through, and with, the eyes of Spirit.

Each of us has different gifts of sight. Some photographically record everything they see. Others see shapes, colors, textures, and dimension that many may overlook. Others see that which is invisible. Which best describes you?

WHAT TO DO

1. What is it you are unwilling to look at?

2. How would things be if you looked through the eyes of Spirit?

3. What do you need to see?

FAITH

While on a plane, I got the sense of faith when I looked out the window onto a sheet of billowy white clouds. I **knew** without a doubt that the earth was below the clouds, even though I couldn't see it.

Without thinking, many of us have more faith in a chair than we do in Spirit. We don't think, "This chair is going to let me down if I sit in it." We just sit down, knowing it will support us. How much greater is Spirit's ability to support us than a chair? Let's turn our concerns over to Spirit, trusting we are completely supported.

Faith is the other side of doubt. The greater your doubt, the greater your ability to have faith.

AFFIRM:

I call on the faith deep within to come forth and lead.

WHAT TO DO

1. Sit in the safest, most comfortable chair in your house. Curl up and imagine the chair arms grow and enfold you so you feel safe.

2. Recall or imagine a time when you felt completely protected and safe. Now magnify that ten-fold. Feel how safe and protected you are.

3. Multiply that as much as you can, then know you are always cradled in invisible arms - no matter what.

FAMILY
(*See* FRIENDS, CHILDREN)

I noticed that I treated my family and friends differently. I was kinder and more compassionate with some friends than with my own children. I was more indulgent with my children than with my friends. I wanted to treat everyone equally. I watched my behavior and my limits and brought them more into alignment.

Do you treat your family differently from the way you treat your friends? What would be different if you treated friends like family and family more like friends? Would you be more involved in getting to know family members on a new level? Would you trust your friends more if you treated them like family?

If your family members neither believe in you nor support you, perhaps you have a circle of friends who can serve as family. Are you part of someone's family? Are you there for others?

AFFIRM:

My spiritual family supports me and I support them. We were divinely joined to express the best in ourselves.

WHAT TO DO

1. Write out the qualities of members of your family you admire. Have you developed those qualities?

2. Write out the qualities of the friends you admire. Have you developed those qualities?

3. Whom would you like to include in your circle of friends? Invite them.

FATIGUE
(*See* RELAXATION, POWER)

Much of my life was spent being "exhausted." I was running on my auxiliary tank, feeling exhausted and pushing myself beyond human limits. I was weary from worrying, obsessing about the past, future obligations, and constantly measuring my performance and myself. I felt I had to be a perfect wife, mother, employee, student, friend, neighbor, volunteer, musician, seamstress, cook, Brownie Leader, etc. It was exhausting. I felt I had to do it all myself. What a bunch of false information!

Sometimes I still want the world to see how hard I work – I act as though I can get extra points for effort. Being raised during the "work ethic" era where working hard and supporting your family was the noble thing to do, has left its earmark. Silly phrases like "idle hands are the devil's workshop" have imprinted me so that I need to work extra hard to allow myself down time to rest, relax, and just have fun.

It took years to give myself permission to do nothing on a vacation. I thought to have a great vacation, one had to sight see, do volunteer work, or tackle a big project. What a new concept it is for me to do nothing.

I remember daydreaming as a child. When my teacher would call on me, "Judy, what are you doing?" I was too ashamed to tell the truth, so I'd say, "I'm considering possible answers." When my parents called through my bedroom door, "What are you doing?" I answered, "I'm reading," or, "I'm doing homework." Saying, "I'm doing nothing" didn't go over well in my house. There was an unwritten rule to be productive at all times.

Part of me still buys into that because I find myself looking at the clock to figure what task I can accomplish in the 20 minutes I have before an appointment.

Negative thoughts exhaust the body as well as the soul. Rest your mind on the powerful, the wonderful, the beautiful, the sweet, and see how good you feel.

AFFIRM:

There is a power that dwells within us that has all the strength and vitality necessary to complete tasks. We are energized, alive, enthusiastic, and alert. Breathe in deeply to release this inner power and puff out any weariness that lingers. Stretch out your arms and lift your chest to fill your lungs with renewed energy. Be restored, and be grateful.

WHAT TO DO

1. Notice any negative self-talk in your head.

2. Notice which tasks tire you out and which ones energize you.

3. What signals does your body give to alert you to stop and rest? Does it request you sit down, close your eyes, and take deep breaths?

4. Slow down, catnap, rest your eyes and do what is necessary before exhaustion sets in. Decide ahead of time how you will respond when you feel tired.

5. Can you take on fewer projects or get assistance?

6. Give yourself more time to complete tasks, and avoid interruptions?

FORGIVING
(*See* FREEDOM)

My younger years were spent hating the people and circumstances that hurt me. I clung to the belief that I was right and everyone else was wrong. I decided I was the good heroine in my story of life.

During the time I would **not** forgive, I glued myself to the persons and situations I hated, so I became a prisoner to the horrible memories I wanted to forget. When I forgave, (gave up my need to be right), I freed myself.

At this writing, I'm in a relationship that gives me trust and freedom to work my way through past issues. I feel as though I'm a veteran with post-war distress syndrome including flashbacks. With each situation that comes up, I need to remind myself that my beloved is different from any past experience. He is not here to hurt me, take advantage of me, or frighten me. He is here to stretch me into my greatness and just love me. I'm touched by his patience and his willingness to create safe spaces where I can expand and express myself.

AFFIRM:

Today, I let go of resentment. I harbor no negative thought. There is no place for this in me because the power of the Living Presence that dwells within does not judge. When there is no judgment, forgiveness is never needed.

God accepts us as we are, dirty diapers and all. Let's also be generous and accept others and ourselves just as we are.

WHAT TO DO

1. How might God look at you and others? Look through those eyes.

2. Look at the 12 Step recovery workbook. Pay attention to steps 4,7,8 and 9.

3. Write out how your life would look if judgment no longer existed.

FREEDOM

A man had been wrongly imprisoned for eight years. On his release, an interviewer was baffled because the prisoner was not bitter. The prisoner explained, "I had a choice to look up at the sky and feel free or look down at the mud. I just looked up."

I am humbled when I see beyond my little self and realize I live in a free nation, I have every possibility open to me, and the only limits are the ones I place on myself. I am free. People, places, and situations do not bind me. Only my thoughts and behaviors limit me.

So why is it that we think we have few or no choices? Because we don't know what we don't know. In other words, we can only see the prison we've created and do not realize that we aren't seeing beyond the prison walls to unlimited possibilities.

AFFIRM:

I dare myself to move out of the prison I've created and step into the unknown world of possibilities.

WHAT TO DO

1. Notice how and when you limit yourself. How has holding on to old beliefs served you?

2. What do you need to release in order to change?

3. Drive a different route to work, see a movie you wouldn't normally see, take a mental health day from work, and hike in a local park.

4. Lift your thoughts to see a bigger picture of freedom.

FRIENDS
(*See* FAMILY)

I've released two dear friends in two years. I never thought I could let a friendship die, but I did.

One friend wanted me all to herself. I felt something subversive and weird was going on. I confronted her and she denied anything was going on. When I felt stalked, I decided to let the friendship die from mal-nourishment.

The other friendship ended because I extended my boundaries way beyond my comfort zones by allowing this friend to stay with me without contributing to the household. I carried her until I got very uncomfortable and angry enough to kick her out. I felt she betrayed me by not being fair. She felt I should have spoken up. We were both right.

The sense of betrayal was stronger than my desire for friendship. I put a bookmark in the friendship. When she called for a status report, I realized that as much as I cherished her, I would not trust her enough to enter into a friendship again. Both situations felt very painful because I have a value to be kind and not hurt others and a deep belief that friends should last forever.

What I've learned is that friendship does not mean giving up healthy boundaries. It means taking care of yourself first and giving attention and love to those around you. One girlfriend taught me about boundaries by showing me how definite her boundaries were. She was clear about what she required for her health and welfare.

What has your behavior taught your friends about your boundaries? I used to think that being a good friend meant that I had to say "yes" to everything that was asked of me.

I have learned that looking good to others is no longer important.

AFFIRM:

Today I choose to demonstrate my friendship by being true to myself. I behave in loving ways because I choose to, not because I have to.

WHAT TO DO

1. Ask friends how you can best demonstrate your friendship to them.

2. Convey to your friends what you would like from them and ask if they think you can give them that.

3. Define what friendship means to you and discuss this with your friends - everyone may have a different view of what being a friend means.

4. Become the kind of friend you desire to have.

5. Let each friend know how much you appreciate her or him.

GIFTS

While doing some deep, inner healing, I became angry with God for allowing me to endure pain and abandonment during childhood. I cried and pounded my fist into the arm of the chair. I wrote God a letter recounting major upsets when I felt threatened and abandoned. As I cried, I asked, "God, why did I have to endure all that?"

At the end of the letter, I felt inspired to write a letter back from God to me. As my pen moved, I had the sensation that words were coming through me rather than from me. God explained that this was the way I learned compassion, understanding, and wisdom so I am able to touch lives the way I do. God also reminded me that indeed I had endured what was placed before me; in fact I had benefited.

As part of this letter, a list of 50 qualities poured from my pen, which I identified as specific gifts that I got as a result of my experiences. These qualities are the tools I use to bless and heal the planet. I put this list of gifts on my altar so I can review it daily.

AFFIRM:

Today, I give my special gifts to the world. There are things I can do that no one can do in my special way. I honor and use the talents I've been given to make this a better world. I choose to be a blessing in the hearts of those I meet. I give thanks for my gifts.

WHAT TO DO

1. Look around your world and notice what needs to be done.

2. Where can you give your gifts?

3. What are you willing to share with others?

GRATITUDE

When I was 14, I was painfully shy. One remarkable gym teacher saw promise in me. She believed in me. She saw the swan in me rather than the ugly duckling I saw. She encouraged me to enter a speech contest. She coached me through each phase of practice. I entered the contest and immediately froze into silence. She fed me a few lines until the stun of being in front of an audience subsided. I walked away with first place, but none of that mattered. What mattered was that because a teacher believed in me, I was able to face down my fear of public speaking. The semester ended soon after that.

I was too shy to thank Miss McMillan for the extra time and effort she had invested in me, so I decided to tell her how grateful I was when school reconvened in September. I practiced my little speech of gratitude to give her. I looked for her the first day of school. She wasn't there. I went to the office to ask where she was. I was told she had died in an accident during the summer. She was so young and healthy, it never occurred to me that she could die. My heart was filled with remorse that I hadn't thanked her. She never knew how she had changed my world.

I vowed from that moment forward I would always tell people in the moment what they mean to me because I might never get the opportunity again. Miss McMillan's death changed the way I show gratitude, and each time I tell her story, I believe it changes other peoples' lives too.

Gratitude is a grace from Spirit. A heart filled with deep appreciation shows the presence of God.

AFFIRM:

Today, I am grateful for each person and incident that molded my life. Who I am today is a result of every experience. The harsh experiences taught me the most. I bless them all with love. I am not afraid to tell people how much they mean to me. They may never know unless I tell them.

WHAT TO DO

1. What are you grateful for?

2. List those people to whom you are grateful.

3. Tell them and show them how you feel.

GRIEF / GRIEVING / SERVICE

As a young mother, I was acquainted with the children and their mothers on our block. One neighbor had two daughters. Our children were close friends. One day, one of her girls ran into the street and was killed by a car.

Although I didn't know what to say or do, my daughter and I went over just to be with them. The remaining child and my daughter played quietly and I just sat and let the grieving mother cry and tell me the story of what happened over and over. I truly didn't know what to do or say. I just sat and listened. Years later, that mother told me our gesture to come and sit with her made all the difference in the world. Other neighbors did not show up, which deepened her sense of loss and separation.

When someone is grieving, just show up. You will be doing a great service just by your presence.

I read a story about a man who came to a grieving family and quietly shined everyone's shoes for the funeral. A simple gesture, but he showed up and performed a kind deed. The shined shoes were a gesture of his love.

AFFIRM:

Today, I ask, "Spirit, how may I serve you?" I assist others because I'm led to do so. I do not have to know their deepest needs. I don't even need to know how to help them. I show up because my nature is to give care and love. Spirit helps me ease the way for others. I serve because it is in my heart to do so.

WHAT TO DO

1. Ask Spirit what needs to be done.

2. How can you best serve?

3. What are you willing to do?

4. Even if you feel awkward or uncomfortable, do it.

GUIDANCE
(*See* PRIORITIES)

Do you want to hear a strange phenomenon? I seek guidance yet I don't like to be told what to do. That is like shooting myself in the foot. The benefit is that it has led me to rely on inner guidance. I do believe there is a balance between when we need outside support and when we need inner knowing.

My best friends are the ones who empower me to use my personal strength and are lights showing the way by their own accomplishments.

Through the years, I've heard people say, "Judy, I thought about you and wondered what you would say or do in this situation." Some say, "I thought of calling you, and before I picked up the phone, I saw things differently." We guide others by living our own lives. We may never know all the people we've been models for.

AFFIRM:

Today, I ask for direction. My prayer is affirmative. I say, "Thank you, Spirit, for showing me how." I get direction each step of the way.

WHAT DO TO

1. Sit quietly and ask Spirit for direction.

2. Write down three things that need to be done - prioritize them.

3. Take the first priority and break it down into three further steps.

4. Create a work plan and take action for each step.

HEALING

How many times have you heard that the body heals itself? We have all seen evidence of this ranging from a tiny scratch to gaping wounds and serious diseases. Our job is to support our body with wise choices. Sound information tells us we need to eat fuel food, exercise, rest, keep ourselves clean and well groomed, and lovingly care for our bodies.

Likewise, our mind heals itself with compassion and love. Past memories do not have to haunt us. We can put them down and decide to stop telling ourselves the story about what happened to us. What happened just happened. What we tell ourselves about it keeps our story alive. It keeps us feeling the same way about ourselves and about life. Let it go once and for all and step forward.

AFFIRM:

Today, I know I'm in Spirit's hands. I have no thing to fear. I accept exactly where I am. I know it is a temporary situation. I am led to people and places that support my healing. I believe in miracles, so I allow the healing energy of the Great Healer to touch me and make me whole.

WHAT TO DO

1. Ask Spirit to direct you to those people who can best support you.

2. Ask your body what it needs from you.

3. Visualize energy flowing through your body to the places that need healing.

4. See yourself totally healed and in perfect health.

HOME

Home is a feeling in our heart, not necessarily a physical place. Home is a heart connection with those we cherish. It is a sense of well-being and security from knowing we are dear to our loved ones. Home is what we create from our outpouring of unconditional love.

I always thought the tortoise had the perfect idea of home - he took it with him wherever he went. A friend who lived in many places as a child, confided that when his fiancée asked where home was, he answered, "Here with you."

My best friend, Geri, had a beautiful home. She was immaculate and everything is in its place. If someone made a mark on her table or spilled something on her white carpet, she didn't fuss at all. She made everyone feel so comfortable and at home that she was nearly invisible as she cleaned things up.

My friends call my home Planet Judy because it is bright, peaceful, beautiful and serene. I chose to create a serene environment because the homes I grew up in were unkempt, unloved, dirty, and dark.

I think our home says what we think about our world and ourselves. What does your home say?

AFFIRM:

Today, I know that wherever I go, I am home. God is always with me, so I am guided and protected. I bring a sense of safety and warmth to all that I meet. I give unconditional love; so wherever I go, I am received with unconditional love.

WHAT TO DO

1. Define what home means.

2. What changes will create a feeling of a real home?

3. Do special people represent home to you? What are their qualities?

HURT

My tender heart and thin skin seemed to be a curse because unkind words or deeds easily wounded me. I felt deep pain for people, for animals, as well as all living things - plants, trees, and flowers.

There is another side. I see that a thin skin and a tender heart have a great capacity to receive joy and love. We can love faster, deeper, longer, and richer. While others experience joy, we experience jubilance and ecstasy.

AFFIRM:

Today, I have an invisible shield around me. Only good and loving thoughts come to me. No thing in me needs to be hurt. I let go of any false belief that pain serves me. I am open to see whatever gift is revealed by this situation. My experiences no longer require pain. I know that no one can hurt me without my permission. I am sturdy and strong.

WHAT TO DO

1. Declare, "Nothing in me needs to be hurt!"

2. Finds ways to keep yourself safe in the future.

3. Feel your strength protecting you.

IDEAS

I have always believed that everyone is filled with wonderful ideas waiting to burst free. Ideas flow when we are clear of limiting thoughts and mind chatter. Humans are built to create ideas. It is called problem solving. Our desire to solve problems is so strong that we even create problems in order to solve them because we are bored.

A distinguishing feature among successful people is that they activate their ideas. Ideas are just words describing a wish until they are put into action. It is like describing how you will paint a picture. All the words are empty. The finished painting says it all.

We have wonderful ideas. The saddest thing is that we don't activate them so they just aren't being used.

AFFIRM:

Today, I let Divine ideas flow through me. I know that all ideas are from the Great Creator. Loving ideas seem like gifts from the angels. I accept them and move into action those that will be of service. I ask, Spirit, what would you have me know and do today?

WHAT TO DO

1. Read *The Artist's Way* by Julia Cameron.

2. Draw an imaginary circle with a dot in the center. Pretend you are the dot and your mind is the circle. Now enlarge the circle and enlarge it again. Each time you allow new or different ideas to flow, your mind is expanded. There is NO limit.

JEALOUSY

I was a jealous wife. I fell in love with Dave when I was 17. He was so beautiful in my eyes. He had curly red hair, freckles, brown eyes, was tall, muscular, funny, and he was my prince. I was certain he was as attractive to everyone else as he was to me. Years later we married and ironically he left me for another woman.

However, my jealousy had nothing to do with him or our situation. My jealousy was my own belief that I was not enough – was not enough to hold him. Although I was very attractive, I was only invested in being what I thought he wanted as a perfect wife. What I failed to be was the real Judy Winkler, with my vulnerability, fears, desires, passion, imperfection, and humanness. It's hard being married to Mary Poppins – practically perfect in every way.

So today, when my beloved doesn't call or see me when I want him to; when his other priorities take precedent, I get a twinge of fear that I'm not enough to hold him and he will leave me. I quickly remind myself that if he chooses to leave, I will feel sad and perhaps feel very empty for a while. However, I will create an empty space for someone else to fill who will be just perfect for me.

AFFIRM:

Today, I know that everyone is in his/her right place. I am Spirit's child in whom the Creator is well pleased. I am fine just as I am. Those who choose to be in my life are here by Divine appointment. There is nothing I need to do or say to keep anyone whose time it is to move on. Actors will move in and out of life's play. Spirit has a plan that is already cast. Above all else, I remember to be kind to myself. Acceptance during times of change makes life less painful.

WHAT TO DO

1. Enroll in a self-esteem course.

2. Do these exercises:
    a) Every time you look in a mirror or look through a window (including the car window), say to yourself, "I, (your name), am lovable and capable."

    b) Each time you go through a door, say, "I, (your name), accept change."

KINDNESS
(*See* ACCEPTANCE)

The suicide note read, "I've been in this town two weeks. Every day I walk to the bridge but no one smiles or says hello. Today, if no one smiles or says hello, I'll jump."

We don't know how powerful a smile or kind word can be to someone. Don't hold back; give your smile away easily. Speak words of kindness whenever you have that opportunity. You may not only be brightening someone's day and giving out hope; you could be saving a life.

My dear friend, Leslie, lived in my condo complex. She struggled with cancer. I shared information about alternative treatment, brought her books and supplements to try, talked with her about attitude and positive thinking. During the past two years, she had surgery and chemotherapy. She was in New York a number of months each year for treatment.

While she was away, I tended to her plants and monitored mail that came her way. I wrote to her weekly. I kept her up-to-date with homeowner information and sent her things I thought would amuse and cheer her up. Even though she never responded, I kept writing.

After about four months, her brother called and told me she was in the hospital and was not expected to live. A week later, Leslie passed away. He thanked me for my kindness and asked me to tend to legal business for him in California, which I was thrilled to do. He put her condo up for sale. I did as much as I could for him before he and his wife came out to pack up and liquidate Leslie's estate.

He asked me what he could offer me for my kindness. I asked for Leslie's two violet plants. He insisted my children take valuable household items.

I did acts of kindness because that's who I am. The gifts my family got were unexpected and frosting on the cake.

AFFIRM:

Today, I allow my inherent nature to flow from my heart out into the world. My kindness is spontaneous and anonymous whenever possible. My kindness is like a footprint of joy that is left wherever I have been. My thoughts, words, and actions make a difference.

WHAT TO DO

1. Smile and acknowledge everyone you see.

2. Respect and consider each person as if he or she was God in human form.

3. The more unlovable a person is, the more he or she needs your kindness.

4. Leave anonymous notes and flowers whenever possible.

LISTENING

I always dreamed of being a charismatic conversationalist. I pictured large groups gathered around me, as though they were parched desert nomads drinking in my words. That never happened. Instead I developed my listening skills. What I've learned is that gifted conversationalists are informative, entertaining, and inspiring. Good listeners heal the heart and lead people back to their own souls.

Which would you prefer to be?

AFFIRM:

Today, I am silent and use my wonderful listening skills. I listen with my heart so I hear the message beneath the words. I stay present and careful not to judge, argue, nor refute. I am given the perfect words at the appropriate moment to respond. My intent is to use words that speak the truth while neither harming nor controlling others. My listening makes a difference.

WHAT TO DO

1. Practice listening with your heart.

2. Listen between the words to hear what the person means.

3. Feed back what you heard and felt. Check to see if your input was accurate.

LONELINESS

Although I might easily be called a hermit because I enjoy my own company, at times I feel lonely for my beloved. I miss the safe harbor of his arms, the laughter, the kisses, and the deep communion of our souls – that space where I can no longer tell where he begins and I end.

Our commitment is that we stand for each other, are here for each other. When our work or projects keep us apart, I feel an ache of loneliness. I know that each of us is blessing and healing those around us. I remember I was whole before I met him, I am whole now, and I shall be whole should we end our commitment.

There is a balance between not depending on others to make us happy and being open and vulnerable to the impact of those who are dearest to us. I've been on both sides of this coin. I've been independent as well as totally dependent. I was sure I would die if my husband left. I lived through my greatest fear. He left and I'm still alive.

AFFIRM:

Today, I know that I can never be alone. I am a spiritual being, the beloved child of God, who dwells in me. Spirit is my breath, my heartbeat, my hands, feet, my creative talent, and my voice. Spirit carries me when I feel I cannot walk another step. Spirit guides and protects me. The wind kisses my cheek, the grass tickles my feet, and the splendor of nature fills my soul. I am one with the Infinite Spirit. Oh Mother earth, Father sky, Brother tree, Sister flower, we are one.

WHAT TO DO

1. Write about your experience of loneliness as a child. What belief about yourself resulted from your experience?

2. How have you sustained this belief about yourself?

3. What do you need to release in order to move forward?

LOVE

Last year I contemplated the word "love." My expectation was a mental picture of a prince charming type or perfect mate with all the attributes I appreciate. Surprisingly, as I went to a deeper level of silence, I was stricken with an overwhelming emotional response. Tears flowed as my heart poured out rivers of love and gratitude. My understanding was that God's greatest act of love was to implant in each of us a yearning to know Him - a desire to go home to the Creator. I saw love in a new light from that moment on.

Our one great desire is to love and be loved. We look for it in the outer life instead of beginning on the inner plane. We start by knowing we are loved unconditionally. We activate this by loving ourselves unconditionally and doing what is necessary to keep self-appreciation and self-acceptance flowing. It takes practice.

When you think or say unkind or unloving things about yourself, stop and release those thoughts. This will make a tremendous difference in the way others see you and treat you. I wore an invisible sign, "It's okay to kick me because I don't think much of myself." A policeman told me rape victims have a predictable profile. Their walk reveals they have low self-esteem and are fearful people. Now my invisible sign reads, "Love is welcome here." People can read our invisible sign.

AFFIRM:

Today, I am open to love. I love myself. I am loving. I am lovable. I am loved.

WHAT TO DO

1. What does your sign say?

2. Contemplate the word "love." What did you discover?

3. When do you feel most loving? When do you feel most loved? How would your world look if love prevailed?

MARRIAGE

I see marriage as the cross bar of a goal post. Each partner is like a pole in the ground, providing equal support. A marriage cannot stay in place if either post will not support it. Here's another image: Picture a pyramid. You and your mate are at opposite base points. The marriage is the top point representing the highest of both of you.

Being in partnership with another may not be an easy road – particularly if you are spiritual partners helping each other stretch into your full potential. Bumps occur. On the road, we call the Auto Club for help. In marriage, counseling can get us fixed up and moving on our way again.

The more deeply we commit ourselves to a spiritual marriage, the more everything else will come up and hit us in the face. In other words, whatever needs to be healed in us will be revealed to us. It is shown so we may correct and heal it. It may not be what we would prefer or want at the moment. Without your partner, you could not be all you are meant to be. Bless him or her daily for your growth.

AFFIRM:

Today I thank my partner for being in my life. He/she is stretching me into the person I was born to be. I show my gratitude by acts of kindness and keeping a grateful and generous spirit, regardless of what is happening inside me or around me.

WHAT TO DO

1. Recognize that Spirit gave you the perfect partner to help you stretch and grow into the person you were meant to be.

2. Realize that your marriage problem isn't about your mate, rather something in you that needs attention. What needs attention?

4. How would you be if you were suddenly transformed into the most loving, caring, devoted partner? What is keeping you from acting that way now?

5. Get professional help when needed.

MY MAGICAL SELF

Each of us has a magical self. Our eyes and ears delight in everything when we pretend to see and hear them for the very first time. Let your imagination run wild. Be enchanted by the impossible, stirred by the brave, humbled by the courageous. Dream the impractical. Think the absurd and life will be fun and magical.

My beloved took me to a restaurant we had gone to when we first became friends. I remembered that evening and how awkward I felt. It was like being on a first date. I felt shy and didn't want anyone to hear our conversation. At our next stop, we stood in line at a dessert restaurant and he touched my shoulder and back as though we were a couple instead of friends. Although it felt natural because we were such good friends, I felt uncomfortable because this wasn't supposed to be a date. I moved away and tried to make small talk, which I do not do well.

The magic happened weeks later when we discussed shifting our friendship to a deeper level. It opened up possibilities that were not present before. It feels wonderful to be open, vulnerable, and available to all of life's sensations – the sounds, flavors, colors, and tastes.

AFFIRM:

Today I welcome newness and changes. I am able to handle whatever life brings.

WHAT TO DO

1. Take a small child for a walk and see everything through his/her eyes.

2. Eat Jell-O with your fingers.

3. Make up a fairy tale.

4. Read *Living Juicy*, by Sark

5. Imagine that you rule a kingdom, describe it in detail.

6. Buy silly slippers and wear them.

MY PLACE

I want you to know this is critically important: You are a player in a Divine plan. You were created at this time for a very specific reason. Your past experiences gave you special coping skills, while your talents and gifts are your tools to express the person you were born to be. You play a part in healing the planet in a way that only you can. Please remember this.

Your place is established by who you are. Your value in your place is established by how much of yourself you give into life. The richest man in the world is he who has the most to give.

AFFIRM:

Today, I claim my special place in the world. I have a right to be here. Even though the universe will continue to operate without me, my presence is important. I am the missing piece to life's puzzle.

WHAT TO DO

1. Read Values on page 153 of this book to remind yourself who you really are.

2. Visualize a tunnel with your name on it. As you walk into the tunnel, you will see a time line with pictures that show each time you used your gift. What would it look like? Describe it in detail.

3. If you ruled the world, how would you change things?

OPINIONS
(*See* BEING ME)

I heard a minister say, "If you are afraid of what people will think, then say nothing, do nothing, and be nothing."

A friend told me of an imaginary idol called "Wuddle." She said we pray to it all the time – "Wuddle (What'll) they think? Wuddle they say?" Aren't we driven by what we imagine someone else may say or do?

Imagine you were free to be yourself all the time. Most of us were engineered to be people-pleasers. It is painful to think that not everyone loves us. It is a stretch to remember that other people's opinions and their beliefs have nothing to do with us. They are making a statement about themselves and their belief.

AFFIRM:

Today, I rely solely on Spirit's opinion of me. What others think, say, and do have nothing to do with me. I am God's precious child in whom the Father is well pleased. That's all that matters.

WHAT TO DO

1. Ask Spirit what you need to do to get on with your work.

2. Write down what comes to you.

3. Take action.

PATIENCE

My ex-husband was a very impatient driver. He would not wait in any kind of traffic jam. He would prefer to drive on sidewalks rather than sit still. I drove very conservatively and cautiously.

However, once I drove very fast to make up for my lack of planning. I was annoyed when traffic slowed down due to a traffic accident. I suddenly got it — I could have been that accident had I not been "off schedule." I, in fact, was on Spirit's schedule and I was kept safe.

AFFIRM:

Today, I let Spirit's perfect time unfold. I see the gifts presented to me by each delay, detour, or obstacle. Spirit has the details orchestrated perfectly.

WHAT TO DO

1. Ask Spirit to reveal a new way to handle impatience and frustration.

2. Consciously decide NOT to react to anything, but take your time to respond.

3. Write down situations that trigger impatience. Decide ahead of time how you will handle each one. For example, I don't like to be kept waiting so I ask my friends to call me when they are ready to be picked up.

PEACE OF MIND

It is my belief that the greatest gift I give to others, as a minister, coach, friend, and mother is to remind them that all is well and whatever they are feeling is just fine and whatever is happening is okay. It isn't the situation that throws us. It is our belief that we need to be different from the way we are.

We get into trouble because we run our old tape that who we are is not ok and we should be another way. No, who you are is just fine.

The 23rd Psalm is read at the moment most people yearn for peace of mind. Here is my understanding of it:

The Lord is my shepherd; I shall not want. **(Spirit assures me that I am cared for.)**

He makes me to rest in green pastures; he leads me beside still waters. **(Spirit provides that which nurtures and balances my life.)**

He restores my soul. He leads me in the paths of righteousness for his name's sake. **(I am given rest then filled up. He invites me to follow him by example.)**

Yea, though I walk through the valley of the shadow of death, I will fear no evil; for thou art with me; thy rod and thy staff they comfort me. **(Spirit is with me so that together we can handle whatever comes along. Spirit has given me tools to use to help me through everything.)**

Thou preparest a table before me in the presence of mine enemies; thou anointest my head with oil: my cup runneth over. **(Spirit demonstrates benevolence and protection. He blesses me beyond measure. I am filled with his abundance.)**

Surely thy goodness and mercy shall follow me all the days of my life; and I shall dwell in the house of the lord for ever **(Spirit continually demonstrates how he blesses, cares, and provides for me. Spirit's love is eternal so I can depend on God's love forever.)**

AFFIRM:

Today, I rest in the safety of the Divine Presence. I am rocked in loving arms and protected from all harm. Peace comes from within and floods my being until I become peace itself. I know that all is well.

WHAT TO DO

1. Be with nature.

2. Say the 23rd Psalm.

3. Sit quietly and breathe. Visualize peaceful energy flowing into whatever part of your body feels tense or needs attention.

4. Notice your thoughts and flow with them, don't try to change them or judge them, and just notice. Focus on your breathing.

5. Put on calming music and let the music come into you.

POWER / STRENGTH

I've never felt more powerful in my life than now. My power comes from three elements: 1) being able to distinguish in the moment how I am being. In other words, I am present to hear my intentions, my words and I am able to listen and really get what the other person is saying so I can communicate intimately; 2) my past no longer affects the major areas of my life. I am conscious when I'm behaving from a decision I made long ago and when I am in the moment I am free; and 3) I no longer need to worry about how I look to others so I am free to see the possibilities in life.

AFFIRM:

Today, I know I have all the strength and energy I need. The source of this power and presence lives in me. My Spirit moves mountains. I shall be given the strength to accomplish what is necessary when it is necessary. I will not let myself down because I can count on my word to myself.

WHAT TO DO

1. Affirm that you will not be forsaken.

2. What does your body need to realize its full potential?

3. Write down what you need to nourish yourself, rest yourself, and strengthen your muscles. Decide ways to accomplish this.

PRAYER

The most profound prayers have come when I begin with "God, my heart is open, come be with me."

Can you see the state of surrender that swings open the door of possibility?

Most of us are concerned that our prayers are not eloquent enough, or that we haven't prayed "right." Just be willing to surrender whatever you've been holding on to; ask for help in your own way. That is good enough.

Prayers, like muscles, develop and become strong through exercise. The more we pray, the easier it gets and the stronger we get.

Our Father who art in heaven, hallowed be thy name.
Thy kingdom come.
Thy will be done, on earth as it is in heaven.
Give us this day our daily bread.
And forgive us our debts, as we have forgiven our debtors.
And lead us not into temptation, but deliver us from evil.
For Thine is the kingdom and the power and the glory forever.
Amen.

The Lord's Prayer is given to us as an example of HOW to pray. Be creative and be yourself.

AFFIRM:

Today I pray to strengthen my bond with Spirit and to strengthen my spiritual muscles. My prayers are mostly gratitude for who I am and what I can give to others.

WHAT TO DO

1. Create a prayer journal. Record your requests and answers to prayers.

2. Pray at least two times a day.

3. Develop your own method of prayer.

PRIORITIES

Contemporary life is demanding. It is easy to get overwhelmed. We use electronics, calendars and project plans to keep us on track. A daily priority task list brings plans into action in the present moment. But there is something beyond the daily tasks that is the glue that holds all our projects together and a ribbon that binds all of our life experiences together. It is the bigger picture that may get obscured by all the dust we kick up as we rush through our projects.

We forget that we are here for a bigger purpose—my purpose is to bless and heal the planet by making a difference in the lives of others. That is my priority.

Begin and end each day with time for Spirit, and you will be able to handle everything that comes along.

AFFIRM:

Today, I put Spirit first. I begin and end my day in prayer and meditation. With Spirit first, all things fall into place. I ask Spirit, "What do I need to do now?"

WHAT TO DO

1. Ask Spirit what you need to do first.

2. Create a daily task sheet with columns.

3. Write out what needs to be done with its due date.

4. Put each task in order by date due.

5. When others are involved in your project, make agreements so you are all in synch.

PROTECTION

As a youngster, I wasn't protected by those responsible to keep me safe. I concluded that I was the only one I could depend on to protect myself. I didn't trust others, so I forfeited intimacy.

Reflecting on how I lived, it was like being in a prison with an invisible moat. I dared anyone to try to come close, knowing they would fall into alligator infested waters. What I perceived as protection turned out to be self-imprisonment.

At some point, I began to trust that the world was a safe place and the universe was on my side, not out to hurt me. I drained the invisible moat (although I have one or two alligators in storage), and allowed people to come close. What a difference!

AFFIRM:

Today my purpose is to bless everyone and everything I come into contact with. My job is to serve at my highest level. Spirit protects me so I need not control anyone or anything. That frees me to create and do the work commissioned by God.

WHAT TO DO

1. As you leave your home for the day, mentally surround yourself with the loving protection of the Divine. Say to yourself, "I go with God."

2. Affirm The Unity Prayer:

   THE LIGHT OF GOD SURROUNDS US,
   THE LOVE OF GOD ENFOLDS US,
   THE POWER OF GOD PROTECTS US,
   THE PRESENCE OF GOD WATCHES OVER US.
   WHEREVER WE ARE, GOD IS!

RELAXATION

Did you grow up thinking you get extra points for working harder or faster or smarter? My belief was that if I worked REALLY hard, I was being good. I drove myself like a workhorse. I piled so many tasks onto myself that I would sink into sleep before my head hit the pillow. I wouldn't stop. I was so exhausted that my body broke down. I fainted constantly and I was forced to go to bed to refresh and nourish myself.

While I rested in bed, I fretted about missing work, school, being a good mom. I truly didn't believe it was okay to stop and rest unless I was very, very sick.

A number of years ago, a girlfriend told me how to really enjoy the process of being sick. She said to eat my favorite foods, watch my favorite videos, wear my favorite nightgown, and pamper myself so I really get into being sick. It worked! I let myself be pampered and I got well very quickly. Now I recommend people enjoy being sick and play it full out. It works for them, too.

AFFIRM:

Today, I give myself permission to rest. My soul needs rest to re-connect with Spirit, my friends, and myself. My body requires time to recuperate and regenerate. I listen to my body because it tells me what it needs and when.

WHAT TO DO

1. Take a mental health day from work. Relax in bed, do what feeds your body and soul.

2. What rejuvenates you? What makes you feel rested and at peace? How can you provide yourself with that?

3. Write relaxation time into your daily calendar.

4. Reward yourself with treats and/or special recognition.

RELEASE OF OTHERS
(*See* ACCEPTANCE)

A couple had been happily married for 45 years. The husband died. The wife told me that his death was the most loving thing he could have done. After her mourning period, she realized had he been around she would not have reached out and done the things that eventually opened up her creativity. He had released her to experience areas of her strength she wouldn't have experienced had he lived. What a generous heart the wife had to see the gifts available to her.

AFFIRM:

Today, I know that each of us has a path to follow. Some journeys bring us together to share our gifts. When it is time to move along, we part in love so each of us can be open to our next experience. We are not property to be owned, we are free spirits who have destinies to fulfill. Spirit knows what good is in store for us, so in faith, we let go and allow that to take place.

WHAT TO DO

1. Is there someone or someone's memory you are holding on to? What do you get from holding on?

2. Write how your life would be if you let go.

3. When you are ready, write them a farewell letter and ceremoniously either put the letter in a balloon and release it or burn the letter.

4. If you believe you are psychically tied* to someone, picture yourself cutting the strings. Visualize them floating away.

* A psychic tie occurs when souls make an agreement in another dimension or lifetime. So when a connection is stronger than you believe is appropriate, it is probably a psychic tie.

RESENTMENT
(*See* ACCEPTANCE, PEACE OF MIND)

When things didn't turn out the way I'd expected, I felt upset. My upset went unexpressed, so I became bitter and resentful. My usual game was that I wouldn't guard my boundaries so I allowed others to take advantage of me.

Instead of taking responsibility for my actions, I blamed others. I got to feel like a victim, which felt more virtuous than being wrong for not assuming my own responsibility for what happened. So resentment is an unexpressed upset.

AFFIRM:

Today, I accept responsibility for every upset I have. I see that it is my responsibility to deliver communication when it is called for. I can transform bitterness into acceptance, love, and forgiveness. I have the power within to set myself free.

WHAT TO DO

1. Write a detailed description of your resentment.

2. Who are you making wrong by holding on to this resentment?

3. Imagine love washing over you in warm, wonderful waves. Each wave purifies you until at last you are washed clean of resentment and you are free.

RESPONSIBILITY
(*See* PRIORITIES)

I worked in the corporate world for a long time. During one major corporate buyout, I watched how the stressful situation brought out the best and worst in people. It looked like most people were using their kindergarten coping skills. That is, rudimentary survival skills were practiced just as if they were in a sandbox. Most employees created more problems by complaining and doing destructive behaviors.

The one quality that separated the spiritually mature employee from the others was respond-ability. Instead of reacting with child-like behavior, spiritually mature employees took time to respond in a way that was unemotional and focused on solving problems rather than creating more problems.

My responses were prudent and wise because I sought the welfare of all.

AFFIRM:

Today I do what is best for the highest good of all. God's will prevails therefore; I cannot make a mistake.

WHAT TO DO

1. Responsibility is respond-ability. What do you need to respond to?

2. Ask Spirit for wisdom and insight.

3. Direct yourself to someone who can help you.

RISK-TAKING

Risk-taking is the shortest road to self-esteem. The fastest way to gain confidence is to step through fear. I've been a passenger in an aerobatic stunt plane, done 87 mph on a motorcycle, skied down the face of mountains, and white-water rafted. I've dared to go within to walk through the horror chambers in my own mind and to face down the demons from my past. Each experience brought greater self-appreciation, and respect.

Emotional risks require as much courage such as telling someone you love them or inviting them to join you, risking they will refuse. Keep asking and keep telling people you love them and it gets easier.

AFFIRM:

Today, I dare to step into the unknown. Each risk stretches me into more of the person I am meant to be. Risk-taking empowers me and builds confidence. Spirit directs each step and will be there to catch me if I fall. I become more alive with each risk I take.

WHAT TO DO

1. Write down what keeps you from taking a risk.

2. List what you think would happen if you risked.

3. Decide on one risk and do it.

4. Record in your calendar what risks you take and their results.

5. Ask Spirit to accompany you through each new experience.

SAFETY

Since most of my life felt unsafe, I devised techniques to be able to function. Back then, I believed I had to control situations and people around me so I wouldn't get hurt, feel scared, or feel helpless. Freedom came when I began to trust that Spirit handles everything and everyone for me. That liberated me to get about my life to serve at a higher level.

AFFIRM:

Today I step into the world knowing it is waiting for me with open arms. This is a safe place for me to be. God is my protector, my guardian, my anchor, and my advisor. I am safe.

WHAT TO DO

1. Know that Spirit will NOT let anything come to you that you cannot handle.

2. Wear an invisible shield that only good and love can penetrate.

3. Memorize the Unity Prayer:

    The light of God surrounds me,
    The love of God enfolds me,
    The power of God protects me,
    The presence of God watches over me,
    Wherever I am, God is!

4. Step out into the world.

SELF CARE

Airline safety advises when oxygen masks are needed, secure your mask first, then your child's. How true this is. We cannot help another until we help ourselves. When we give ourselves what we need, we set an example for those around us.

Recently I was part of a self-mastery team. I asked the team how I might support them. One player said I already support him because I inspire him by sharing my experiences and allowing him to witness my changes.

AFFIRM:

Today I care for myself as if I was caring for Spirit, for God dwells at the core of who I am. I lovingly listen to my needs and fill them the very best I can.

WHAT TO DO

1. Write out what you wanted from your parents when you were a child. Did you need to be listened to, encouraged, comforted, kept clean or dressed nicely?

2. Decide on ways to give yourself what you need today.

3. Become the parent you always wanted.

SELF REALIZATION

I completed a growth process this year. To get the most from the program, I required of myself that I own being a jerk. In other words, it was necessary to identify persistent behaviors and sneaky games I play with people – without making excuses. My whole pattern has been to keep looking good and not let anyone see that I'm imperfect. Now I feel liberated. I can set down the mask of perfection and be Judy Winkler – with all my flaws.

This has made a huge difference in how much closer I feel to others and them to me.

We are spiritual beings incarnated in physical form. Our bodies, which are filled with our personal values, special gifts, and talents, were given to us so we could bless and heal in our own special way. Doing God's will means that we recognize our values, gifts, and talents and use them. We must recognize how special we are and not hesitate another moment. We are the missing piece in life's puzzle. Let's get about doing our heavenly work.

AFFIRM:

Today, I acknowledge that I am the beloved child of God. I exhibit each heavenly quality I have inherited.

Today, I may be the closest thing to God that someone will ever know. Therefore, I let my divine qualities shine so brightly that I become the lamp that lights the way for others.

WHAT TO DO

1. Spend time with people who cherish and nurture your spiritual essence.

2. Meditate and pray for ways to express your gifts.

SONGS TO SING

As a child on a Tennessee farm, I loved to listen to a farm hand whistle and sing. Work seemed fun and easy and his tunes seemed to add joy to everything. Today, I love to hum and sing. It is a sure way to lift the heart.

Notice the tunes you absentmindedly hum. Perhaps they have a message for you.

AFFIRM:

Today, I sing out. Birds don't sing because they have perfect pitch or belong in a choir, they sing because they have a song. Today, I sing because I have a song. My heart is filled with music to share.

WHAT TO DO

1. Sing, whistle, hum.

2. Create songs or rhymes as you do your tasks and take your daily walk.

3. Tell Spirit in words or song how you feel about the world.

TRUST

As I've mentioned, as a child, the grownups in my world were not trustworthy. I protected myself by placing an invisible shield around me so I wouldn't get hurt. Carrying a heavy shield is hard work and there wasn't much energy left to be myself. After a while, I became the shield.

No matter how thick the shield or how long we carried it, or why we needed it, it will be discarded in a blink of an eye when we feel safe enough to let it go.

AFFIRM:

Today, I rest in the knowledge that Spirit protects me. No harm can come to me. I am guided with ease so I come to life with an open heart and open mind. It is safe to be me.

WHAT TO DO

1. Can you trust yourself? Do you keep your word to yourself?

2. Decide where you can trust more.

3. Discuss trust with your friends.

UNITY

When people come for coaching, the one constant factor is that they feel separated from Spirit. They become upset, and then seem to give themselves "time out" and isolate themselves from Spirit. It is like sending ourselves to our room until we can behave.

From my vantage point, all of life's drama is because we are out of harmony with Spirit. We have two positions: we are in harmony (unity) with Spirit or we are out of harmony (separated). Notice when life runs smoothly and roughly, then draw your own conclusion.

If I step off my spiritual path, life fills with pain, but Spirit within urges me to return home. So I'm drawn back into unity again. When I remember I'm God's child, well protected, loved, and guided, I feel at home.

AFFIRM:

Today, I know there is one power, one source of all good that is Spirit. Whatever we choose to call Spirit, Spirit *is* Spirit. Just as all the elements of the ocean are in one drop of ocean water, the power that is in Spirit is in everyone, therefore is also in me as Spirit. Spirit in me keeps my life running smoothly—this is my spiritual pacemaker.

WHAT TO DO

1. Meditate on the oneness of all life.

2. Write what unity means to you.

3. Find a flower or leaf and carry it with you for a week. Contemplate unity with all living things.

VACATION
(*See* RELAXATION)

I once allowed a platonic friend to join me on a trip because I didn't want to hurt his feelings. My real feelings surfaced the first day we arrived. I was a disagreeable companion. I shut down and didn't want to be cooperative, and found I took my feelings of resentment with me. I felt sorry for myself and I ruined part of my holiday time. In a day, I did an attitude change, apologized and made the rest of the trip fun.

Wherever I go, I take myself with me. Before I leave, I am sure that loose ends are tied up, the work is done, the house is in order, and I am mentally free to take in the good waiting for me.

Mini vacations are healing and revitalizing. They can be as simple as breakfast in the hills nearby. Short day trips can be lovely and refreshing.

AFFIRM:

Today, I change scenery to experience new adventures. My choice is just right for me. I allow all the good to come to me. Everyone I meet is blessed by our encounter. I just show up and have a good time.

WHAT TO DO

1. Ask yourself what you WANT from an experience. Decide how you might get it.

2. Is there someone you'd like to invite?

3. Plan time away, even if it is only for a few hours. Treat it like an exotic vacation.

4. Prepare, go, and enjoy.

VALUES
(WHO AM I?)

We must first know WHO we are before we can be true to ourselves and live in alignment with our values. Focus on who you really are. Remember why you were born. <u>You</u> are the gift that you bring to the party of life. You make all the difference in the world.

From the list below, which values do you cherish and hold sacred? Which values would people use to describe you at your funeral?

ACCOMPLISHMENT: reaching goals, seeing results
ADVANCEMENT: progress, headway, promotion
ADVENTURE: excitement, thrill, new risks, variety
AESTHETICS: beauty, balance, color
AFFECTION: love, caring, fondness
ALTRUISM: aiding others, improving society, serving
COMMITMENT: 100% devotion
COMPETITIVENESS: striving to win, being the best
COMPLETION: starting and ending a project before moving on
COOPERATION: teamwork
CREATIVITY: self-expression, imagination, inventiveness
ECONOMIC SECURITY: financial protection,
ENVIRONMENT: acceptable surroundings
FAMILY: close domestic relationships
FRIENDSHIP: close relationships, camaraderie, rapport
HEALTH: mental and physical well being, fitness
HUMOR: fun, laughter, high spirits
INDEPENDENCE: autonomy, liberty, freedom
INNER HARMONY: serenity, peace with self and others

INTEGRITY: honesty, sincerity
INTIMACY: affection, love, amity, bonding
INVOLVEMENT: a sense of obligation, community participation
JUSTICE: a sense of equanimity, fairness
LEADERSHIP: guiding, being in front with ideas and vision
LOYALTY: allegiance, fidelity, dedication
NATURE: drawn to wilderness, spending time outdoors
OPENNESS: vulnerability, accessible, willing to let others in
ORDER: systematic, organized, create routine
PERSONAL DEVELOPMENT: enriching self, growth, reaching potential
POWER: authority, influence, prominence
PRIVACY: solitude, seclusion
RECOGNITION: acknowledgment, appreciation
RESPONSIBILITY: accountability, reliability, ability to respond
SELF-RESPECT: esteem, faith in oneself and abilities
SPIRITUALITY: devotion, belief in a higher power
TRUST: knowing one is safe and one's environment is safe
WEALTH: abundance, prosperity
WISDOM: insight, enlightenment, applying knowledge

WHAT TO DO

1. Mark the 10 values that best describe what you hold sacred at the core of who you are, (even if you don't exhibit them).

2. Now choose 4 of those 10. Prioritize the 4. That will identify who you are at your spiritual center.

3. Ask Spirit to show you how to use these values to fulfill your life's mission.

WEIGHT

I was underweight until I got pregnant, then I stopped being active, and then I got older. Weight crept up and I carry excess weight at this writing.

If we all know how to lose weight, why don't we? Weight is not about food. It is about control, not being controlled, loneliness, anxiety, pain, fear – it is not about a physical hunger or physical food at all.

AFFIRM:

Today, I use food as fuel to energize my body. My body is Spirit's vehicle to do spiritual work. I make wise choices that support my health and well-being.

WHAT TO DO

1. For under eating or over eating, call Over Eaters Anonymous and attend at least 6 meetings.

2. Buy their literature and read it.

3. Get a sponsor.

4. Do the 12 steps of recovery.

WISDOM
(*See* CHOICE)

Did you ever meet a child who was more like an old lady or an old man? I was born old. I knew things children shouldn't know. I heard the unspoken, saw the unseen. I had an uncanny way with animals. I didn't realize that I was different from others until much later in life.

Each of us has innate wisdom. We DO know, down deep inside, what is prudent and what is wise. Our responsibility is to acknowledge and trust our wisdom so that we can act on it.

AFFIRM:

Today, I possess all the wisdom I need. I make wise choices. I pray over decisions and take the time necessary to make wise choices. I can always re-choose so I am reassured that my choice is perfect for today.

WHAT TO DO

1. Write down what would happen if you acknowledged your wisdom.

2. Write down the wisdom that you have kept hidden from the world.

3. Share this information with a trusted friend.

4. Ask Spirit to reveal ways you might use your wisdom.

WORK RELATIONSHIP

Do you have one person at work that rubs you the wrong way? Do you ever think life would be great if that person disappeared? Notice that he or she will disappear as soon as you heal the relationship within yourself.

Those who seem to be the biggest nuisance help us heal something that needs to be healed. They are sent to us to help us grow.

AFFIRM:

Today, Spirit is my employer and in charge. I appreciate the diversity of people in my work environment. I bless all with whom I come in contact. My strong spirit and personal integrity silently set an example. I speak my truth kindly and lovingly. I politely ask for what I want. I have the most fun when I play well with others.

WHAT TO DO

1. Ask Spirit what you need to learn from your current work relationships.

2. Is there something you resist doing and saying?

3. What is the thorn in your side showing you about yourself?

4. Bless and pray for that person daily. Notice how the relationship shifts.

WORLD PEACE

Peace begins with me. I pray that the world's greatest resources become peace, joy, and love. My mission is to model reverence for all living things, to empower, inspire, support and educate so people know themselves and express at their highest level.

AFFIRM:

Today, I am responsible for world peace. I begin with the peace in *my* world. I am conscious of my thoughts of acceptance, non-judgment and unconditional love.

Thoughts are things and my peaceful thoughts actually create peace around me. I live in a peaceful way. Everything I think, say, and do blesses and heals.

WHAT TO DO

1. What is your mission?

2. Write it out and keep it with you.

3. Tell as many people as you can.

4. Demonstrate peace in all your actions.

5. If you do NOT feel peaceful, stop and breathe until you feel the love of Spirit pulsing through your body reminding you that all is well.

APPENDIX

SUGGESTED READING

Alcoholics Anonymous

Drawing the Larger Circle, Jack and Cornelia Addington

Heal Your Body, Louise Hay

Homecoming, John Bradshaw

Inspiration Sandwich, Sark

Key to Yourself, Venice Bloodworth

Live the Life You Love, Barbara Sher

Living in the Light, Shatki Gawain

Living Your Life Out Loud, Rasbery and Selwyn

Love is Letting Go of Fear, Gerald Jampolsky, M.D.

Quantum Healing, Deepak Chopra, M.D.

Seat of the Soul, Gary Zukav

Teach only Love, Gerald Jampolsky, M.D.

The Bible, George Lamsa translation

The Dance of Anger, Lerner

The Four Agreements, Don Miguel Ruiz

The Integrated Being: Techniques to Heal Your Mind-Body-Spirit, Sharon Lund, Ph.D.

The Peace Pilgrim

The 7 Habits of Highly Effective People, Stephen Covey

Twelve Traditions of Overeaters Anonymous

You can Have it All, Arnold Patent

ABOUT THE AUTHOR

Judy Winkler is a teacher, and public speaker dedicated to making a difference in the world through her daily contacts as well as projects, programs, and books.

For over 25 years, she has taught life-changing personal growth classes, seminars and workshops.

She counsels clients to achieve their personal goals while they live with joy and ease.

Her interests include painting, writing, calligraphy, ballroom dancing, gardening, and sewing.

Judy lives in San Diego and has three children and three grandchildren.

CPSIA information can be obtained at www.ICGtesting.com
Printed in the USA
LVOW100453130612

285551LV00001B/5/P